T0373059

# John
# Haynes

# John Haynes

## THE MAN BEHIND THE MANUALS

**NED TEMKO**

**Haynes Publishing**

First published in 2020

All rights reserved. No part of this publication may be reproduced, stored in a retrieval system or transmitted, in any form or by any means, electronic, mechanical, photocopying, recording or otherwise, without prior permission in writing from the publisher.

A catalogue record for this book is available from the British Library

ISBN 978 1 78521 685 5

Library of Congress catalog card no 2019957269

Published by Haynes Publishing,
Sparkford, Yeovil, Somerset BA22 7JJ, UK
Tel: 01963 440635
Int. tel: +44 1963 440635
Website: www.haynes.com

Haynes North America Inc.,
859 Lawrence Drive, Newbury Park, California 91320, USA

Designed and typeset by James Robertson
Printed and bound in Malta

# CONTENTS

# FOREWORD

It was a perfect, pink September evening in Somerset. But that's not the main reason Annette and J Haynes – the wife and eldest son of one of the most improbably successful entrepreneurs in British history – would, half a century later, remember it so vividly. It was because John Harold Haynes, ordinarily the most placid of men, was truly, unmistakably, almost volcanically angry.

And the target of his fury goes to the heart of what drove Haynes – from his days as a mere toddler, on a tea plantation in the thick, green hills of 1940s' Ceylon, right up until his death, shortly before his 81st birthday, on an English winter morning in 2019. It's key to unlocking what helped him not only succeed as a businessman but also join that rare breed – like Henry Ford with his Model T, or Steve Jobs with the Apple Mac – who so viscerally connected with the millions who bought into the innovation he was selling, and who so perfectly caught the moment, that he became not only a success, but a cultural phenomenon. And it is also essential to understanding who Haynes *was*.

Because John Haynes was angry at a car.

To be fair, it was not just any car. It was an AC Cobra. Nowadays, the Cobra is nothing less than an automotive icon. The first of the roughly 1,000 that were built, from 1962 to late 1969, was recently sold at auction in the US for nearly *14 million* dollars. Yet from the start, anyone with even a nodding interest in automobiles recognised it as something special: the marriage of sylphlike beauty and raw power. A classically sleek, low-slung, open-topped British two-seater that pulsated with the muscular growl of an American Ford V8.

Haynes, of course, had far more than a mere nodding interest in cars. Even by this early stage in his life, he'd bought and savoured dozens of them: MGs and Minis and Triumphs, big-bodied Fords and Jaguars, and stately Rolls-Royces. He had raced cars, too, nearly every weekend, until he'd ended up in the hospital just weeks before his wedding to Annette in the summer of 1963. His Lotus spun out violently on the race circuit at Goodwood, near the south coast of England, hit a bank, flipped over and hurled him out straight onto his back.

Yet even a decade later, his *passion* for motor racing remained. He still thrilled at getting behind the wheel of an especially fine, fast car. He had never before driven a Cobra, much less owned one. But he learned in 1973 that one of his old weekend-racing friends owned not just one Cobra but two, and might be willing to part with the one that he wasn't using to race. Haynes wasted no time in deploying every tool at his disposal – mostly raw persistence, allied with a fearsome natural charm – to get the deal done.

And so on an early September morning, John, Annette and their son, J, then only six years old, found themselves purring 100 miles northwards in one of the old Rolls-Royces, through the Somerset countryside, skirting Bath, into Gloucestershire and finally, a few miles past the market town of Stroud, easing to a halt outside a lovely brick cottage in the village of Edgeworth. It was home to A.C. Brown, an accomplished amateur racer and all-round motor enthusiast known to his friends as Tony. And it was home, too, to his pair of AC Cobras.

Once the formalities were done, Haynes set off home in his sleek red Cobra, with J strapped into the passenger's seat beside him and Annette following in the Rolls. Neither father nor son said a word as the roadster hurtled along the old Roman roads of Gloucestershire. J could barely see above the dashboard, but that didn't matter. Enveloped by the roar of the V8, he was mostly watching his father's face: beaming with excitement, the smile almost beatific, as if he'd reached the automotive equivalent of the Promised Land. Which was what made what happened after they got back home all the more jarring.

'It handles like a pig!' Haynes fumed when they got out. 'I don't understand for the life of me why everyone makes such a fuss of this car. It's terrible!'

It wasn't until after dinner that he skulked back outside to have another look, more and more frustrated, and hugely disappointed. It was Annette who suggested that he might want to check the tyre pressures. When he did, first the front, then the back, the smile returned. One of the tyres was at a mere 15psi, another at 24psi, a third at 30psi and one of the rear ones at 40psi. Crouching down, he pumped each of them up to the proper pressure. Getting back in the driver's seat, he pulled out of the drive, turned onto the main road, and sped away, returning a half-hour later grinning broadly. Not only did he never regret the purchase. When Brown phoned the following week, having had second thoughts about selling the car and wanting to buy it back, Haynes was polite but firm: 'Sorry, Tony. But no.'

The Cobra purchase came at an especially important juncture in Haynes's life. Even though he was in his mid-30s, it marked a kind of dividing line between an elongated youth – and a business adolescence as well, in which he'd seized opportunities, played hunches and ridden a mix of extraordinarily good judgment and good luck – and his entry into fully fledged adulthood. Parts of the younger Haynes would always remain: the engaging mischievousness, the appetite for risk-taking, the underlying sense that some way, somehow, things would turn out for the best. That's one reason why only a vanishingly small number of the many thousands of people whose lives crossed with his in the years that followed had a single bad word to say about him.

But both his business and his personal lives were fundamentally changing.

The business – Haynes Publishing, with its soon-to-be-iconic catalogue of car repair manuals – had only recently set down more permanent roots. Its various tentacles – taking apart the cars, photographing them and putting them back together; writing and printing the first generation of manuals; and selling them along with an assortment of other motoring titles – had been divided between a combination office-and-bookshop in Odcombe, which John's younger brother, David, initially outfitted as a contract printing business, and a garage-and-printing operation that John had set up in the converted barn at Camway, the rambling old house he and Annette had bought in the nearby village of West Camel when she'd been pregnant with J. But not long before buying the Cobra, Haynes had formally moved all the operations into a former creamery a few miles down the road in Sparkford. It would remain there for all of his life.

The family was now a settled unit, too. J's younger brother, Marc, had been born in 1968. The third and final son, Chris, was nearing his first birthday. And to all but a handful of people, the 'adult' John never ceased to appear anything but self-confident, sprightly, sunny, and successful.

And he *was* all of this. The smile – soon to be wreathed by a beard he grew, shaved off; then grown again and come to love – was genuine. His business successes were dazzling: Haynes manuals thrived not just in Britain but were poised to start tapping a critically important, larger market overseas, in the US. As a husband, he was always aware of his remarkable good fortune in having married Annette. She was not only a tireless mother to their children, but a ready partner in whatever hijinks he still occasionally suggested they get up to: what David described as 'working hard, and playing hard'. And from the outset, she was also an indispensable part of the Haynes business operation.

He was a loving father, too, though the physical affection he showed to the boys when they were very young – the 'tickle-fests' and the made-up stories his sons would remember all their adult lives – faded as the children grew older, before making a comeback in his later years as a grandfather. In short, John Haynes was one of those few people of whom it could be said that the inevitable plaudits following his death – from friends, employees, and the obituary-writers – rang absolutely true.

But they missed something as well. Not something dark. Not something that belied the obituary praise. Yet something essential to understanding not just the John Haynes experienced by those he met and lived and worked with, but an intensely private part that existed alongside the bonhomie, the fondness for social occasions, the enjoyment of public attention, and that radiant smile.

For there were two discontents which Haynes would carry with him in the years that followed that Somerset evening in September 1973.

The first never troubled him to the point of distraction. It was more akin to the slightly over-loud whir of an old refrigerator, something you always figured you'd get around to fixing, but which you got used to. The roots went back to his teenage years, when he had adopted the formidable William Richard Morris as his hero.

Morris was the one-time bicycle-repairman who went on to build the vast Morris automobile empire, giving the motoring world, among other defining products, the Morris Minor and the MG Midget – and who, for his industrial success and equally titanic philanthropy, would be knighted, as Viscount Nuffield.

He received a basketful of other honours as well: five honorary law degrees, and honorary fellowships at four Oxford colleges including Nuffield, which he had founded and endowed.

To a remarkable extent, Haynes did end up following the Morris roadmap, taking an initially improvisational business idea and building it into a worldwide commercial empire. Though he became rich, he, like Morris, shunned the personal excesses of others with many millions in their bank accounts. While he never amassed anything like Morris's wealth, he did endeavour to use his fortune to help others, not just through his business or for his own family. He endowed a world-leading international motor museum just down the road from Sparkford – with his own, ever-growing private collection of vintage cars as its initial centrepiece.

Yet with all this, there was always a sense of slightly unfulfilled ambition – even after being awarded an OBE in 1995 for his services to the British publishing industry. 'He, quite literally I think, saw Morris as his idol and example,' his brother David remarks. His sense was that John was never fully satisfied that he'd measured up to that exalted mark. Haynes did not crave Morris's wealth; nor even his knighthood, or any other of the specific honours bestowed on him. It was vaguer, more general: an aspiration of something nearer to the weight and breadth of Morris's reputational heft, a desire to leave a legacy. That was one reason, in his later years, that the motoring museum that bore his name assumed ever greater importance to him.

Haynes never said this outright, but a hint that his public accomplishments mattered to him could be found at the family home. Framed, in the downstairs loo, were his own OBE, as well as the honorary degree he was awarded a decade later, by the Open University.

And also framed alongside them was a signpost to his other closely guarded source of discontent: the words of *Desiderata*, the gently idealistic guide to life and career written by the Midwestern American poet Max Ehrmann on the eve of the Great Depression in the 1920s. It ended with these words:

> With all its sham, drudgery, and broken dreams, it is still a
>   beautiful world.
> Be cheerful. Strive to be happy.

Haynes's second discontent sorely taxed that maxim. Unlike the quiet urge to equal the heights of Lord Nuffield, it was not just a matter of droning background frustration. It was a deep, and deeply hidden, pain. And it was in 1973, the year of the Cobra, that it became inescapably clear to him that there was nothing at all he could do – no bright new business idea, no new strategy or acquisition, no appeal to higher authority – to make things right. It concerned his middle son. Around the time of Marc's second birthday, he'd been diagnosed with a rare, debilitating spine condition. The ailment led to a succession of visits to doctors and hospital wards, then to a series of operations, and finally, in 1973, around the time of his fifth birthday, he was confined to a wheelchair.

Marc's first few paraplegic years were the hardest for Haynes, as he counted down the time his son had left. The prognosis was that he would live, at most, into his teens. What made it even worse at first was something obvious to everyone in the family: Marc, among the three boys, was by far the most like John. He was delightfully mischievous. He was strong-willed. Far from being daunted by whatever challenges lay in front of him, he was ever eager to take them on, and somehow defeat them. Over time – as he not only made it into his teens but well into his fifth decade, not only inheriting his father's enthusiasm for cars but, amazingly, even finding a way to race them – John grew to feel a special love for Marc. He felt a sense of wonder, and raw pride. Still, the pain never left him completely. It was made all the more difficult because he kept it buried inside.

Only very occasionally did he talk about it to Annette. Never did he speak of it to others, even close friends or family.

Still, true to the words of Ehrmann's poem, he *did* 'strive to be happy'. And when all was said and done, he succeeded – not only in that, but in making others happy too. Through his Haynes motor manuals, he touched the lives of more than *200 million* people around the globe. Nothing in all of the words published in newspapers or on websites after his death better captured that connection than the torrent of unsolicited messages posted on the company's Facebook site.

Yet what probably would have most delighted Haynes himself – though he always remained almost comically disinclined to embrace the Internet age, receiving email messages only in printed form through his secretary, scribbling his thoughts in longhand and getting her to key in the replies – was an extraordinary tribute on YouTube. It came from Scotty Kilmer, an American whose own unlikely path to success was a bit like a twenty-first-century version of Haynes himself. A second-generation auto mechanic from upstate New York, Kilmer began posting wonderfully informative car-related videos in the summer of 2007. By the time Haynes passed away, Kilmer had nearly two million subscribers, and had clocked up more than *half a billion* views. Though the two men had never met, he posted an effusive six-minute celebration of the Haynes manuals – how they came to be and what made them, and still make them, so special. He pronounced John Haynes 'the most important man in car repair history'.

But Haynes was more than that. He didn't just sell car repair books, and those who bought them weren't mere customers. Haynes's story is also a defining part of the story of Britain during the final decades of the twentieth-century – just as Steve Jobs and his computers have been intimately entwined with another kind of social transformation during the first decades of the twenty-first-century. Or Henry Ford, during the late 1920s and 1930s, in depression-era America.

'Someone should write an erudite essay on the moral, physical, and aesthetic effect of the Model T Ford on the American nation,' the Nobel Prize-winning writer John Steinbeck wrote, in a mix of lyricism and gentle irony, in *Cannery Row*, his novella of life and love and laughter in 1930s Monterey, California. 'Two generations of Americans knew more about the Ford coil than the clitoris, about the planetary system of gears than the solar system of stars. With the Model T, part of the concept of private property disappeared. Pliers ceased to be privately owned and a tyre pump belonged to the last man who had picked it up. Most of the babies of the period were conceived in Model T Fords and not a few were born in them.'

So it was with John Haynes and his motor manuals. They were inseparably part of a time, beginning in the 1960s, when Britain's post-war austerity and post-imperial decline were beginning to be overtaken by a new spirit of possibility, self-confidence, energy. Two trends, in particular, embodied the change. One, like Henry Ford's Model T, involved the internal combustion engine. Many millions of Britons – mostly but not only young men – became car-owners for the first time. Part of the transformative effect on their lives was practical: they could go across their towns or cities, or across the country, to visit friends, enlarge their experiences or, crucially, to find work. But the deeper change was psychological. It gave them a new sense of themselves: not just a feeling of freedom, but of control, and self-worth. There was one thing a great number of these new motorists *didn't* have, however: the money to spend on getting a professional garage to fix their cars when something, inevitably, went wrong.

But a second trend was becoming evident as well: Britons' discovery of the satisfaction, and financial benefits, of do-it-yourself improvements and repairs in often-drab post-war apartments and homes across the land.

What Haynes did was to tap in perfectly to these twin changes, and to marry them together. By producing his motor manuals

– literally disassembling pretty much all of the most popular brands of automobiles; putting them back together again; meticulously photographing every step; and then explaining in plain language what all the component parts did, and how to fix or replace every last one of them – Haynes created generations of amateur, DIY automobile car mechanics. And *amateur* is the right word: because the millions of people who bought and used his manuals discovered real love, real joy, in the power Haynes gave even the least naturally mechanical of them.

'Rest in peace,' read one of the Facebook messages sent on the day his death was announced. 'My passion, my obsession, my love of cars started with the purchase of a simple Haynes manual, which quickly became the bible of my life, giving me the knowledge to support and fuel my determination and build my dreams.'

Another said, simply: 'Great geezer! Thank you.'

Yet what makes Haynes's story especially compelling is that the idea for his motor manuals didn't emerge fully formed. It wasn't a product of business school, or consumer focus groups. Just as the roots of Steve Jobs's Apple Mac can be traced to his personal urge to build the most perfect personal computer he could imagine, Haynes's journey began when, as a teenaged schoolboy, he was dead set on figuring out how to turn the remains of an old Austin he'd found in a scrap yard into a fully working sports car. Then, a few years later, on how to take apart and fix the ailing Austin-Healey of a Royal Air Force friend on a trestle table a few miles from their base near the Arabian Sea.

It all could still have ended differently, of course. Returning to Britain at the end of his RAF posting to Aden, Haynes could have gone on to serve as a gradually more senior desk officer in the air force, taking his generous pension and retreating into serene retirement. But that didn't happen. And to understand why, you have to travel back more than 30 years, and 5,000 miles, from the Somerset September when he first got behind the wheel of his AC Cobra.

*Chapter One*

# CHILD OF THE EMPIRE

If John Haynes missed the distant South Asian island where he grew up, or missed his parents, whom he would see only fleetingly during his teenage years, he never said so at the time. But both mattered enormously to what he became, and what he accomplished. He understood that. He valued it. He even made a stab at writing about it, in a family memoir which he began, but never got very far with, decades later.

He was a child of the British Empire. He was born on 25 March 1938, in the Hatton Nursing Home. It was a simple, three-storey medical centre. It had been founded in the 1800s, like the town of Hatton around it, to serve the British planter population in the hill country of what is now Sri Lanka – then, the British colony of Ceylon. At first, the planters had grown coffee, and they hacked their way through nearly 400 square miles of pristine rainforest to make Ceylon one of the world's leading producers. But an outbreak of fungal disease in 1869, blighting pretty much the entire crop, marked the beginning of the end for the coffee farms. By 1900, tea plantations had replaced nearly all of them. By the time Haynes was born, millions of tea plants – each row planted precisely a metre apart, and looking from afar like vast, lush-green swathes of carpet – scaled the hillsides in the island's interior. The picking was done mostly by Tamil labourers, ferried across the narrow gulf from south-eastern India. If you were British in 1930s Ceylon, you likely either owned one of the tea plantations, or you helped manage them.

John's father was listed as an 'assistant manager' in the employment records for most of the nearly half a century he spent in Ceylon. Yet at the height of his career – from the mid-1920s until around the time John turned four years old in 1942 – he was actually a lot more than that. He oversaw a number of the estates owned by one of the major British tea enterprises, the Waitalawa Group, in an area spanning nearly 3,600 acres. And a year before John's birth, he was formally promoted – only briefly, as things would turn out – to overall group manager.

The story of John's parents was as extraordinary as his own. His father, Harold Haynes, was the youngest child in a well-off family in Essex; not far, nowadays, from Stansted Airport.

Harold's father, and his grandfather too, were GPs. But as he made his way through school, he showed little interest in medicine, nor, for that matter, in any sort of further studies. At 16, he found a post as a junior clerk in the City of London, a job he endured more than enjoyed. When the First World War broke out, he wasted no time in volunteering.

Like many thousands of others, he was still under enlistment age. But they sent him to the trenches in France with a unit called the City of London Volunteer Rifles. Just a few months later, he went over the top with a few dozen of his comrades, stumbled into a shell-hole and was grazed by a bullet from a German sniper. As the others retreated, Harold blacked out. When he came to, he lay immobile until nightfall, but managed to crawl and clamber his way back to the British lines, at which point he was taken back to England to get patched up.

A few weeks later, Harold rejoined his unit. Then he was shot again, this time taking a bullet square in the shoulder, and was sent home for good. But he *liked* the military. And when offered the option, he took a desk job until the end of the war with the Royal Flying Corps, the precursor of the RAF.

Had it not been for his spell in uniform, Harold would almost certainly not have ended up in Ceylon. At a pub lunch in London with another of the volunteer rifleman after the war, one of his former trenchmate's friends approached them. 'You were injured in the war, were you?' he asked Harold. 'Well, anybody who's fought for King and country, I'll give a job to. How would you like to go to Ceylon and learn tea-planting?'

So he did; but even that was not straightforward. He enjoyed the training well enough, but he was still in his twenties, and he found the social life in the remote hills – or, more accurately, the *lack* of social life – stultifying. Along with another young trainee, he quit, and they boarded a boat for Australia. Their plan, if you could call it that, was to find work, make money, lots of it if possible, and figure out what to do from there. For a while, things went to plan. They got hired on an apricot farm in the far western corner of Australia, and, with little to spend their earnings on, asked the owner to set aside their monthly wages with an understanding that they'd take the whole sum when they left. What they didn't reckon on was a sudden glut in the apricot market. The farmer went bust, and their wages vanished along with him. For lack of any other option, except the unappetising one of heading back to England, Harold returned – this time, for good – to Ceylon.

The life of the woman he would marry nearly fifteen years later – John's mother, Vi – was the stuff of a Gothic novel. To go by her birth certificate, Violette d'Hennezel was born in 1904 to her German mother, Lena, and French father, Albert Maurice d'Hennezel. But that wasn't true, and, among the Haynes family, only Harold knew the real story until shortly before her death in the late 1980s.

In fact, Vi's 'father' Albert, a successful Paris businessman who travelled around Europe selling fine textiles, was never even aware of her existence. The couple already had an infant daughter, and while Albert was on his business travels, Lena often took months-long sojourns to England, where she stayed with various friends. At least one of them, in 1903, had become especially friendly. Vi was born the following year, in a handsome, red-brick home in Chiswick, West London. The child's biological father, an expatriate American businessman working in the City of London, continued to stay in touch and helped with financial support, until returning to the US several years later. Yet two weeks after the birth, Lena entrusted her baby to the foster care of a woman named Helen Hayward, who was the daughter of another one of her London acquaintances.

Lena was not prepared to lose little Violette completely, at least in the beginning. She arranged with Mrs Hayward and her husband, Richard, to pay five shillings a week toward the child's upkeep for the first five years of her life. Lena seemed hopeful of gradually building up the courage to tell her husband what had happened, and then bringing her daughter back to Paris. She continued to visit the Haywards every six months or so, posing as a family friend, laden with gifts for the Haywards' own three children and a special present for her daughter.

But shortly before Vi's fifth birthday, everything changed. First, Richard Hayward died of a sudden illness, leaving 39-year-old Helen with barely enough money to feed and care for the children. Then, Lena – and her financial support – disappeared. Maybe it was because she and Albert had now had a second child of their own, a son, and she decided not to risk his finding out about her London daughter. Still, the rupture with Vi would have happened anyway. A couple of years later, the entire d'Hennezel family perished in the devastating flooding that hit Paris in 1910.

Mrs Hayward moved with the children to a cold-water tenement in south London. With her own health also increasingly delicate, she took in sewing work, and did stints as a caretaker for wealthier homeowners, to make ends meet. With both of Vi's elder step-siblings now more independent – the eldest, Edie, having left to train as a nanny, and stepbrother Percy with a job in a nearby Boots – Vi became close to the youngest, Maudie, who, at seven, was barely a year older than she was. They went to school together every morning, and they especially enjoyed the weekly ritual of Sunday school classes at their local church. But Vi was becoming more and more highly strung, and difficult to manage – in part, Maudie would later be convinced, because she'd somehow learned that the absent Lena was her real mother. Not long after Vi's seventh birthday, the local vicar persuaded Mrs Hayward to send her away: to a Dr Barnardo's children's home in Northampton, with the understanding that all contact with her foster family would be broken.

Vi was now, for all practical purposes, doubly an orphan.

She also proved amazingly resilient. In her mid-teens, she managed to breach the Barnardo's rules and get a postcard to the Haywards, and they offered to take her back. But after more than seven years away – and the accumulated traumas Vi had endured – the reunion was not easy for either side. She did briefly move in with Edie, who was working as a live-in nanny for a large and fairly well-to-do family, but that was never going to prove a lasting arrangement.

So at sixteen, she applied for a nursing course at St James's Hospital in south London. Since she was below the age qualification, she was put on the waiting list, but she was accepted upon turning eighteen. In going on to qualify as a nurse, as well as a midwife, she found not only a new sense of security; her work also gave her a sense of purpose, and a source of pride. It became not just a job, but a vocation.

Then, after Vi moved to a post at the NHS hospital in the old Essex market town of Bishop's Stortford, north-east of London, a twist of luck – for once, *good* luck – changed her life beyond recognition. Of the hundreds of people she had cared for in her first few years there, one in particular – a woman in her late thirties, named Amy Haynes – had become a lasting friend. In the spring of 1935, Amy invited Vi to to join her for tea at the old Regent Palace Hotel, off Piccadilly Circus, along with her mother and her older brother, one Harold Haynes, who was on a six-month furlough from his job managing tea estates in Ceylon.

There was a bit of a sense of high-school dating, for both of them, during those first few months. With Vi working during the week, she and Harold met every weekend. They went out to meals together, and to parties. They played tennis, too, with Harold pointing out hopefully that there was a court just down from his bungalow on the tea plantation. Yet they were both inexperienced, and awkward, at courtship. And whether because of his natural shyness, a real concern about whether he could offer Vi a fulfilling life in the hill country of Ceylon, or a fear of being rebuffed, Harold left at summer's end for the three-week boat voyage back home without mentioning, much less proposing, marriage. Vi, who was upset at the way they'd parted, had no such doubts. She was certain they belonged together. And while she knew she couldn't simply abandon her nursing post, pack up and leave, she did crave the opportunity to begin creating what she herself had for so long been denied: a strong, and stable, family. As things turned out, she needn't have worried. Harold held out for all of a week. When the boat stopped off at Port Said, on the Suez Canal, he wrote her a letter asking her to marry him.

And she did. Not immediately. For nearly two years, they sent each other letters: sometimes more than once a week yet, with airmail services still in their infancy, sometimes taking three or four weeks to arrive. They wrote with a deep affection, a shared longing to begin their lives together. Harold's letters were full of details about life in Ceylon, plans for a reconstructed bungalow to make her life there more comfortable and, as time wore on, questions about how, and when, Vi would like their wedding to be held. Harold was still worried about how she would adapt – and Vi herself bought a return ticket, just in case. Still, she had no qualms in replying: they should tie the knot as soon as her ship docked in Ceylon.

She arrived early on a Thursday morning, on 6 March 1937. They were married, with a handful of Harold's friends in attendance, at 11:00am at the nearest thing the capital city, Colombo, had to an Anglican cathedral: the Gothic-style Christ Church, a few hundred metres from the waterfront. Harold then spirited his bride off for a few days' honeymoon south of the city at Mount Lavinia – the iconic British hotel, built more than a century earlier as the private residence of the second governor of the colony and perched on a rise above its own private beach. Early the next week, they boarded the train for the sinuous, six-hour trip, inland and upwards, to the refurbished bungalow near Rangala in the centre of the island.

When John Haynes was born almost exactly a year later, it was at the high point of his father's long career in Ceylon. Settled into the hilltop bungalow with his new bride and their infant son, he now finally had the formal title – not just the duties – of overall manager of the Waitalawa group's estates. He was in his early forties. He had every reason to look forward to perhaps another decade in the top job, an expanding family, and then, buoyed by a generous pension, to a comfortable retirement back in England.

Yet by the time his next furlough was due, in the summer of 1940, and Vi was pregnant with their second child, the Second World War had broken out. The fighting had yet to have any impact on Ceylon. The Japanese entry into the war was still eighteen months away, and the fall of the British stronghold of Singapore would not occur until 1942. But the sea voyage back to Britain had become impractical, and Harold decided instead to decamp with the family to Australia. He rented accommodations for them in Perth, just a few dozen miles from the farm where he and his friend had picked apricots twenty years earlier. John's younger brother, David, was born there in November. Early the next year, they all returned to the manager's homestead in Rangala.

It was then that things turned more difficult. Within a year, Harold's sixteen years with the Waitalawa group came to an abrupt end. When he'd first been hired, back in 1926, Waitalawa had only recently been taken over by a larger conglomerate, Ceylon Amalgamated Tea & Rubber. Now, the parent company decided to restructure Waitalawa, bringing in a smaller team of new managers, and Harold appeared to have been a casualty. There was certainly no evidence he'd done anything wrong, or had suddenly become any less good at his job; in fact, he would go on to manage several other large individual estates for other owners. However, the prospect of the full pension he'd counted on was gone, and with it the possibility of settling back in Britain any time soon.

John spent the first thirteen years of his life in Ceylon. It was not a life of great wealth, especially once his father had left Waitalawa, but it *was* a life of privilege. From their perch in Harold's trio of successive manager's bungalows – especially the last one, where he would spend his final decade before finally moving back to England in 1960 – they overlooked the millions of tea plants and the thousands of dormitory-housed labourers who, from dawn to dusk, picked and collected the tea. Some of the local labourers were detailed for household duties: an *ayah*, or nanny, to help with childcare; a cook to prepare all the meals; and others to do housework or odd jobs around the bungalow. They addressed John as 'little master', and David as 'baby master'; Harold was 'master'. He was not just the estate manager. He was a Justice of the Peace, officiating at marriages and, when necessary, funerals on the estate, and a *de facto* magistrate who adjudicated disputes among the labourers and their families when they arose. He was also, at various times, an officer in his regional tea-planting associations.

But for the Haynes children it was an isolating existence as well. There were occasional excursions outside the estate, to nearby landmarks like the cave temples of Dambulla, dating back to the first century BC, or the towering, 1,500-year-old rock fortress in Sigiriya. About once a month, Harold and Vi would take them on a visit to another of the estates, where the manager would sometimes have children of roughly the same age. And at least once a year, the family would spend a few days at Mount Lavinia. But mostly, the children's lives centred on the bungalow, the large garden outside, the wider grounds of the estate. And above all on the family. It was, at least partly as a result, a tightly knit unit.

There was never any doubt that Harold and Vi treasured it. For Vi, who had known life without family, it was what she lived for. But along with their parents' love, which the children never doubted, there was also a kind of formality, a distance. It was not a home full of hugs or kisses, lively banter and conversation. In David's words, many years later, it was a close family, a good family, but never really an *intimate* family. The boys grew up calling their parents 'Father' and 'Mother,' and continued to do so long after they'd left their childhood years, and Ceylon, behind.

Especially when they were very young, it was Vi who provided the ballast in the family. Her Sunday school Protestantism still ran very deep, although her life experience seemed to have taught her to hedge her bets: she hewed to an extraordinary array of superstitions as well. She would begin each meal by reciting grace, a rite she would continue her entire life. Each night, she'd tuck the children into their beds and ensure they said their prayers. Then, as John would later recall in his abandoned family memoir, they would go to sleep 'with the distant hum of music from the radio in the drawing room, while Mother read or knitted, and Father did the crossword puzzle'.

It was Vi who taught the children to read before they began their formal schooling. And she never ceased in her determination to teach them life lessons as well. One evening, when John was about to enter his teens, the family went on a long walk around the estate. Exhausted by the time they returned, John sprawled into one of the upholstered chairs in the drawing room and beckoned a nearby servant: 'Rasu,' he snapped, 'take little master's boots off.' Years later, David could still remember Vi chasing John around the bungalow, threatening to smack him with her hairbrush if he ever behaved like that again.

Mostly, however, she was a source of support. As John's comprehension level improved, she began getting him to read aloud from the daily leader column of the *Times of Ceylon*, having him repeat the longer words until he could pronounce them correctly. She also encouraged the boys to explore – not just physically, romping around, climbing trees and inventing games in the front garden, but also through the written word. John's childhood role model, from about the time he turned seven, became the mischievously dishevelled boy hero of the 'Just William' books, by the English author Richmal Crompton. Vi happily went along with this, insisting only that he abandon the persona and 'dress properly' when they went on visits to other estates, or on their trips to Mount Lavinia.

But especially as John got older, he naturally gravitated more to his father. This was not just because of Harold's role on the estate – the 'big master' managing the work and lives of the labourers who made it run – though he did later recognise that this was a part of it. It was because, through Harold, he could revel in what became, almost from the time he could walk, his real true love: automobiles. The photo of two-year-old John behind the wheel of his first 'car' – his boxy, metal toy roadster – captures it perfectly. His golden locks seem almost to be flowing in an imagined wind. He is hunched forward, with a look of utter determination, almost as if approaching the first corner on a Formula One circuit.

The attraction only deepened. Even as Vi was teaching him to read, John would bury himself in his father's magazines, like *Look* and *National Geographic*, and pore over photographs of impossibly big, powerful American cars. He began collecting Dinky Toys, the iconic die-cast models from back in England. Later, when the family moved to Harold's final estate – Midlands, a dozen miles further inland and upland – he and David built an elaborate dirt roadway for their Dinkies beside the path that led up to the manager's bungalow. It was a few hundred yards up from the tennis court, where the brothers used to race their bicycles. But the highlight of John's day was always when he'd clamber into his father's old, time-worn Austin 8 and join him for the evening rounds of the estate.

And, even as he got older – as the settled life he'd known as a small child faced disruptions, and he became more independent – the fascination with cars always remained a constant.

When John was only five, Vi was suddenly hospitalised; 'Mother is feeling poorly' was all the children were told, though in fact she was suffering from complications from a miscarriage.

Harold was not prepared to turn the boys' care over to the *ayah*. There was no English day school in the vast tea country. So, like a number of planters and managers, he sent them off to a religious boarding school, the Good Shepherd Convent, in the hill-station town of Nuwara Eliya, several hours by train from the estate. To the boys' relief, they were soon brought back home. Their mother not only regained her health. In 1946, when John was eight, she had her third child – a girl, delivered in an English nursing home in Colombo and christened as Mary

Alison Haynes at St Paul's, the Anglican church in the ancient Ceylonese capital of Kandy.

Two years later, however, John and David were again enrolled at Good Shepherd. John's experience there was an unhappy one. For years afterwards, he would remember the nuns as not just strict, but cruel, with a fondness for the sound of wooden rulers on children's knuckles. When he was deemed to have misbehaved – a judgment which, for the nuns, included the slightest sign of boisterousness – they would insist he sit absolutely still for a period of fifteen minutes in the wooden chair at the foot of his bed. He would always recall a kind of dietary torture as well: every meal at the convent school included a large dose of the locally grown bananas known as plantains, leaving him with a lifelong abhorrence of the fruit. Still, he remained there for just a single term, before moving a few miles up the road to The Hill School, the tea-country equivalent of an English prep school.

He liked The Hill School teachers better, but his abiding memories were not of English classes, or maths and science. Every Sunday, the whole student body was packed into a noisy, dank old Hotchkiss coach. For most of the other boys, it was a rite to be endured. But John always looked forward to it. He would invariably get on first and grab the seat immediately behind the driver, following his every shift of gears with wide eyes. The return trip was usually done on foot, along the two-mile road running alongside the lake in the heart of Nuwara Eliya.

On one Sunday, however, he suddenly heard the distant rumble of what seemed to be car engines. Within a minute, the cars appeared – throaty MGs, complete with racing numbers on the side, speeding and squealing, sliding and skidding, as the drivers tried to keep them under some semblance of control. A few minutes later they sped past again. John, with a handful of other willing confederates, stayed for the entire race – at the predictable price of demerits for missing school lunch.

'I was totally hooked on motor racing, from that moment,' he would say decades later. That Christmas, he asked for a model car kit of a Jaguar convertible. It was barely five inches long: a block of wood, from which you had to carve out the body shape; die-cast wheels and real rubber tyres; a windscreen with two tiny bits of Perspex; and stickers to put on the dashboard for the instrument panels. He worked on it for weeks, producing a finished product that looked like it had come out of some minuscule sports-car factory.

Yet John was outgrowing his model cars, his Dinky Toys, and the constraints of tea-country life in Ceylon. As he approached his teenage years, he was endlessly curious. He also had a physical energy that could no longer easily be confined by the tyre-swing Harold had had the odd-job man construct on one of the big trees in the bungalow garden. On one of his holidays from prep school, John commandeered four-year-old Mary's tricycle. Balancing her on the handlebars, and with David jogging along behind, he raced down from the bungalow toward the estate factory where the tea leaves were processed and packed. As he pedalled faster and faster, the trike predictably toppled over. Mary was thrown off and somehow escaped unharmed, to the relief of Vi, almost howling in distress when her distraught daughter rushed back into the bungalow. Yet John, who had moved to cushion his little sister's fall, ended up with a broken arm.

It was obvious to Harold that the boys' future did not lie in Ceylon. Though he had by now spent more than two-and-a-half decades there, he still regarded England as home. But with his reduced pension, he was keenly aware of the need to shepherd his finances. Even sending the boys to the boarding school in Nuwara Eliya had not come cheaply. There was simply no way he could afford to move back with the whole family, much as he was tempted to do so. He did think seriously at one point about a kind of halfway alternative.

On the first of his furloughs after Mary's birth, when John was ten, they'd stayed in a rented house in Hitchin, north of London, near Harold's two older sisters: Bea and the matrimonial matchmaker, Amy. When he returned to Ceylon, he had left Vi behind with the children and enrolled them in a local state school. But the separation was hard on both husband and wife. It took only a few months for them to abandon the idea. Vi removed the boys from school and they came back home.

Now, however, buoyed by a small inheritance from one of Harold's aunts, they began looking at the possibility of sending John and David to an English boarding school. Asking around the tea-planter community, Harold got the names of several that were affordable, as long as he kept working and didn't move the whole family back, and in areas where friends or relations could house the boys when school was not in session. Early in 1951, shortly before John turned thirteen, he finally settled on his choice. One reason was that it had a prep-school house alongside the senior school, which meant that ten-year-old David could attend as well.

With the term due to begin in September, and his next furlough not due until the new year, Harold wouldn't be able to accompany them. And so, on a hot, humid August afternoon, he shook both of his sons' hands on the pier in Colombo and ushered them and Vi, holding Mary close to her, onto the boat back to England.

*Chapter Two*

# TALE OF TWO WILLIAMS

I t wasn't Eton, but Sutton Valence School was barely a century younger. It was initially set up as a grammar school in 1576, under the reign of Henry VIII. It was perched at the top of a pretty little village overlooking the Weald of Kent, about two-thirds of the way from London to England's south-east coast. And it did have an unmistakably public school feel about it: ivy and red brick, an imposing central quad, dapper school uniforms, cricket and rugby fields … and a cultivated pride in being part of a family of 'Suttonians' past and present. It was also undeniably, strikingly, different from anything the Haynes boys had experienced during their childhood in Ceylon.

On arrival in England, Vi and the children had moved in with Noel Newman. He was one of Harold's second cousins, though the boys always called him Uncle Noel. He had a farm in Bottisham, a village east of Cambridge. And that eased the transition, but not by much. The school had laid on a special train from Victoria Station for students coming from London or other points further north. Vi had duly bought the boys their proper uniforms, but the ritual of getting them dressed before leaving for the station was fraught. John's nervousness, which he'd been trying heroically to hide, bubbled over as she helped him into his crisp white school shirt and collar. He couldn't make the studs hold the collar in place as Vi hadn't purchased formal studs for the shirt, assuming the plastic ones that came with the shirt would suffice. The farewell at Victoria was difficult, too. John affected a stoic calm, which David did his best to emulate. But Vi wept unabashedly. She hugged the boys close, as if physically reluctant to see them go.

John's first days at Sutton Valence were not easy. As he'd feared, the other boys, with their screw-in collar studs topped with gold or pearl, sniggered at his plastic substitutes. It was unsettling on a deeper level as well. For the first time in his life, he was utterly on his own. And since he and David would be in different classes, with different friends, in different houses, he would also find himself at an unfamiliar distance from his younger brother.

But over time, he adjusted. In his own idiosyncratic way, he not only coped, but he managed to thrive. Harold had picked the school sight-unseen, but it turned out to be a fortunate choice. John and David were the only 'children of Empire', and there were very few others from overseas. But where the social fabric of a school like Eton drew on nobility and wealth, pedigree and privilege, Sutton Valence was very much part of the Kent countryside around it. A lot of the kids were from the families of local farmers. The nearest thing to a scion of industry was the son of the man who'd founded England's leading manufacturer of roofing tiles. And while Sutton Valence did offer the normal public school menu of maths, art and sciences, Latin and Shakespeare and Milton, it did not see its role, like Eton's, as setting its charges along the primrose path to an Oxford or Cambridge college. It did value academic achievement, but didn't take it *too* seriously – which was no bad thing, because John didn't either.

He had a further stroke of good fortune at the beginning. As a new boy, rather than finding himself in one of the two large residential houses that framed the main quad, he was placed with a dozen or so others in a so-called 'feeder' house. Called Bennett, it was more like a private home, overseen by one of the teachers and his wife. The boys there didn't eat all of their meals in the school dining hall. They got home-cooked breakfasts and dinners around their dining-room table. And the housemaster, a history teacher named F.T.W. Blatchley-Hennah, seems to have provided John with something else as well, a feeling that would be replicated in the close, almost filial, relationships he would go on to enjoy with several other valued faculty members as he settled in at school.

One of them to whom he especially gravitated went by the splendidly public school name of John Bennallack-Hart. He taught biology. He enjoyed cricket and rugby. Yet while John did briefly try his hand at all of these, they weren't the reason that John and he 'hit it off', in David's words. He suspected that it was more because Bennallack-Hart and his softly spoken wife, Corinne, gave John a sense of family, and that John related to Bennallack-Hart, in particular, as a kind of father figure. 'From a very young age, we hadn't seen much of Father, one way and another. And having somebody you saw every day, for three months at a time, you could form a sort of bond.'

But John also revelled in a new kind of independence, especially once he moved from Bennett to St Margaret's, one of the two senior houses alongside the quad. Part of this was the mere fact he was becoming a teenager, on his own, in a boarding school environment. But it was more than that. As he would recall years later, it was the: 'freedom to go where we liked, and do what we wanted, outside of school hours. The time after the roll calls and 'lights out' was unbelievable for a young teenager used to the restrictions of an English-run – "no fraternising with the 'natives'" – tea estate in Ceylon.' He especially enjoyed being able to bicycle wherever he wanted. 'I was always borrowing bikes from the other boys, to cycle into

Maidstone, seven miles away, on sunny afternoons when there were no cricket or rugby games to play.'

What he liked most about cricket and rugby were the days they *didn't* happen. And the St Margaret's housemaster – with another of those wonderful public school monikers, P.S.W. MacIlwaine – seems to have decided very early on to encourage John's preference for two-wheelers, and later four-wheelers, over silly-point fielding and scrums. Even more so than during his early months at the feeder house, he came to value his relationship with MacIlwaine and his effervescent wife, Eileen.

Since John was still far too young to drive a car, at least legally, the bicycle excursions became a high point of his first years at Sutton Valence. They also offered a telling glimpse of the kind of boy he was, and of the kind of man – and *businessman* – he would become. He made only a handful of lasting friends at the school. But his energy, his mischievous sense of adventure, his appetite for trying things with some inner certainty that somehow they'd work out, all of these exercised a kind of magnetism on many of his schoolmates. It was a bit like the circle of children that swirled around young William Brown in the *Just William* books that had so captivated John back in Ceylon. Without it, he'd surely not have found it quite so easy to arrange to borrow bicycles from an informal rota of the other boys.

Still, what John really wanted was a bike of his own. More in hope than expectation, he started setting aside a shilling from the five shillings he got as weekly pocket money to enter a raffle run by the village bicycle shop. At lights out a few weeks later, Eileen MacIlwaine bent down, tapped him on the shoulder and whispered: 'John. You've won the new bike!'

It came with Sturmey Archer three-speed gears. He cherished it. He polished the frame daily. He oiled the gears. At the slightest hint of rust, he applied a special paste he got from the village shop. And when, predictably, his fellow teenage bike-owners began marvelling at the results with a mix of curiosity and envy,

John Haynes set up his first business. Working from dinner until bedtime by the light of a gas-flare lantern, he began giving the Haynes bike-treatment to the other boys' bicycles – at two shillings and sixpence each.

He was not entirely cut off from his family during his five years at Sutton Valence. During his first months there, Vi and Mary had remained at Uncle Noel's farm near Cambridge. They were joined by Harold at the end of the year, when he arrived on his furlough. He found them a house in Elmer Sands, a seaside village on the south coast of England – available because the rental properties there were for summer holidaymakers, though uncomfortably cold because it was, of course, winter.

The family was reunited for the Christmas and New Year holidays. And though the rental house was nearly a hundred miles from Sutton Valence, once school resumed, Harold, Vi and Mary drove up to see John and David on a number of the so-called '*exeat* Sundays', when boarding students were free to go back home. But at the end of the furlough, they returned to the tea plantation. From that point on, when not at school, the boys stayed in Tunbridge Wells, about forty miles from Sutton Valence, with 'Auntie Pat' – the widow of a tea planter Harold had known in Ceylon. An accomplished pianist, she was making ends meet by giving music lessons to local children and by taking in paying lodgers: one of her relatives, one of her friends, and now the two Haynes boys.

As homes-away-from-home, the main reason John enjoyed both Noel's Cambridgeshire farmstead and Pat's sprawling lodgers' house was his still-undimmed love of automobiles. For now, he was left to feed that appetite through the motoring magazines he'd buy at the Sutton Valence newsagent. But on the farm, Noel had happily allowed him to drive around on the tractor. Pat didn't have a tractor. She did, however, have a self-propelled, petrol-engine mower. John delighted in commandeering it to cut the property's lawn, whether it needed it or not.

He also began spending a number of *exeat* days, and end-of-term holidays, in another home, not far from Pat's in Tunbridge Wells. It belonged to the family of his closest school friend, a boy named Colin Furneaux, and a principal attraction was its damp, dank Second World War air-raid shelter. Colin's parents agreed that, since it was unlikely to be of any other use, he and John could begin cultivating mushrooms there. The experiment began unencouragingly. By the end of their first holiday venture, not so much as a single plant had sprouted, and they slammed the door shut in disgust. But when they returned about six weeks later and headed for the shelter to have another go, they were confronted with a veritable mini-forest of mushrooms, which they eagerly picked and sold on to local greengrocers. And so John's second business venture was born, grandly christened Haynes & Furneaux Mushrooms.

Still, it did not take long for the allure of peddling mushrooms, or sprucing up schoolmates' bicycles, to give way to his real passion, for *real* cars. The shift began, quite literally by accident, on a pleasant morning in his second year at school, with the roar of jet engines. A group of Gloster Meteors – British fighter jets, on a training flight – streaked overhead as the boys were walking to the dining hall for lunch. They craned their necks skyward as the jets disappeared into a cloud, only to see the cloud turn red and debris plummet from one of the planes toward the farmland on the far side of the school grounds. As soon as lunch was over, John fetched his bike. With a handful of other boys, he made his way toward the crash site, returning an hour or so later with bits of the jet's remains. Unfortunately, local police officers were waiting when they got back. They had to surrender their haul for use in the investigation.

But John had noticed another artefact amid the debris: the rusting chassis of an automobile. It was a Durant Star – a Model-

T-lookalike that was the brainchild of a fired General Motors executive who was determined, unsuccessfully as things turned out, to give Henry Ford's car a run for its money. Enlisting the help of a half-dozen housemates, he persuaded the farmer to let them take the remains back to school. For months, he nursed and tinkered with the car, eventually getting the engine to work. On an early-summer afternoon, using an upturned wooden crate as a driver's seat, he piloted it across the school grounds and did a ceremonial circuit of the playing fields. But with summer term about to end, the Durant went too. The headmaster called John in and ordered him to 'get that monstrosity off school premises'. He found a local scrap dealer who agreed to cart it away.

Now John's attention turned to a much more ambitious automotive project, born of a visit to the scrap dealer's yard in Kingswood, which was a couple of miles from school. He had his eye on an old Austin Seven – the pre-war economy model fondly dubbed the Baby Austin. Even what was left of the car was beyond his budget. But one of Harold's childhood friends in England had left John a legacy. It wasn't exactly a trust fund – the grand total came to £100 – but it was stipulated that it wouldn't be made available to him until he turned twenty-one.

When Harold and the family returned at the end of 1953 for his bi-annual furlough, John explained to his parents what he had in mind. Since almost all British sports cars were being exported to America, homegrown motor enthusiasts had begun trying to convert the Austin Seven into a sportier, faster, two-seater roadster: the Austin Seven *Special*. John was set on building one of his own. And before heading back to Ceylon, Harold – and, more reluctantly, Vi – agreed to advance him the necessary money from his legacy fund.

He paid £15 for the old Austin. He got the scrap dealer to remove its rusting steel body and leave only the chassis assembly, with the engine and radiator. The village blacksmith helped repair the springs. Then John set about the real work: building a new body from ash, with thin strips of aluminium on the top, and reassembling the engine and the dozens of other components needed to make sure it would actually drive.

If his parents had been key to his being able to buy the remains of the Austin, *building* the Special needed a boost from three other figures who loomed large during John's final years at Sutton Valence. The first two were his St Margaret's housemaster and his wife: the MacIlwaines. They proved perfectly happy to look the other way as his presence on the rugby and cricket fields, already sporadic, dwindled to near-zero. But the third source of support was arguably more important. He was a teacher named Derek A. Simmons, known to his students as Daz. He taught art and woodworking. John liked and admired him, and the feeling was evidently mutual. John's proudest single achievement during his time at Sutton Valence – if you don't count the extracurricular ones, from which he took most pleasure – was winning the school art prize in each of his final three years, and seeing his drawings and paintings enjoy pride of place at an exhibition on school Speech Day. In John's final year, Daz added a special touch: he took a piece of rough-hewn oak and carved a frame for the winner's work.

As John began refitting the Austin, Daz didn't just provide advice when needed; he also arranged for him to be able to work on the car in an area next to the school carpentry shop. John spent much of the last months of his third year on the car. At the end of term, he got a nearby garage to cart it back to Aunt Pat's in Tunbridge Wells, and he kept working on it there. Back at Sutton Valence after the holiday, he drew ever closer to the finish line. And finally, during summer term the following year, his Austin Seven Special was ready.

It was never going to scare the competition at Brands Hatch. The carpentry was more a triumph of determination than practiced skill. Still, it looked the part, with its black-paint finish and wire wheels. It sounded the part, too, with its silencer-less chrome exhaust. And it actually ran. A few days after his maiden venture around the school grounds, Eileen MacIlwaine asked him to take her for a spin. It started well enough, with Mrs MacIlwaine beaming, and dozens of boys watching admiringly, as he drove her around the edge of the playing fields. But about halfway along, the thimble-like pressure indicator on the dash began seeping oil. John got her back to St Margaret's as quickly as he could. He always remained grateful that she affected not to notice the spattered black spots on the front of her crisp yellow dress.

But *building* the car turned out to be a less important signpost to John Haynes's future than what came next. It had been the same with his bicycle. He'd been delighted to get it. He enjoyed riding it, oiling it, polishing it, caring for it. But part of his emerging sense of who he was and what he wanted – away from family, away from the tea estate in Ceylon, on his own – was an ambition to make something *more* of his facility with the bicycles. And, if possible, make a bit of money in the process. From his mushrooms, too. And he didn't even like mushrooms.

He did like – in fact, loved – cars. And he definitely wanted to make more of that. With Daz again urging him on, he decided to type up a detailed account, complete with his own drawings, of how to he had built the Austin Special. It ran to forty-eight pages. Using the school's duplicating machine – an old-style Gestetner mimeograph stencil copier, which you'd hand-crank to run out each page – he produced 250 copies. He folded them into pamphlet form and stapled them at the edge. Then he placed a small advert in one of his favourite car magazines, *Motor Sport*, offering them for five shillings a copy. Within barely a week, he'd sold them all.

And it was not just a spur-of-the-moment thing; it was quite conscious. All the winners of school prizes at Sutton Valence got to choose a book, which they'd receive as part of the award. For his third and final art distinction, he asked for a slim volume by a popular English author named James Leasor, who had written dozens of books, ranging from histories to thrillers. This one was called *Wheels to Fortune*. It was a biography, and the hero was another William. He had begun his working life as a teenage apprentice in a bicycle shop. Then he left, to set up a bicycle-repair business in a shed at the back of his parents' garden. He moved on to building bicycles, and racing them, then building motorcycles. And finally cars. This William's name was William Morris.

How literally John saw his own future path in Morris's is hard to know, just as it is hard to say how he weighed the allure of that future against the importance of everything else he'd learned and experienced as a boy in Ceylon. But he departed Sutton Valence in the summer of 1956 with a pair of graduation gifts: the William Morris biography from the school; and a brown-leather briefcase from his father. He kept both of them for the rest of his life. The well-thumbed copy of *Wheels to Fortune* enjoyed pride of place on his bookshelf. He carried the increasingly scuffed and battered briefcase to work every day, wherever he was, whatever he was doing – refusing, later in life, his sons' repeated offers to buy him a new one.

He left school, too, with an absolute certainty about how he wanted to go about making a living. It was not yet a fully formed idea, but he'd happened onto a formula – the Austin Special pamphlet – and was convinced it would be fun, and profitable, to try to build on it. There was one obvious and unavoidable problem, however. John was just nine months away from turning eighteen, and under the conscription system adopted after the Second World War, and extended in the 1950s during British forces' involvement in Korea, eighteen year olds were required to do two years of national service.

The trick would be somehow to find a way to serve his country without derailing his plans to carve out a niche for himself in the world of cars and those who loved, drove, built and tinkered with them.

*Chapter Three*

# FLYING SOLO

In one sense, John was unlucky. Compulsory national service would soon be phased out, and if he'd been born a mere eighteen months later, he would have avoided it altogether. Still, like so much else in his young life, he'd prove enormously fortunate in the way that things turned out. By the time his RAF tour was over, he would make valued, and lasting, friendships. He would find his first serious girlfriend. And in good part thanks to her, he'd manage to seamlessly combine his day-job – a back-office post on a strategically important air base – with his ever-more-ambitious plans to write, and publish, books about cars.

He ended up in the Royal Air Force almost by default. There were exceptions to the requirement for national service – for coal miners, farmers, or members of the merchant navy – but John was never going to tick any of those boxes. Still, the war in Europe was now over – or at least the *hot* war. So the British authorities did their best to offer conscripts their choice of which branch of the military they joined. The army was never a runner for John. The idea of parade-ground marching was no more appealing than Sutton Valence's rugby or cricket. The navy meant water and, if things went wrong, swimming – something which, if you didn't count paddling around at Mount Lavinia as a child, was utterly foreign to his experience and held equally little attraction. That left the RAF. Poor eyesight, unfortunately, disqualified him as a potential fighter pilot: the airborne equivalent of driving very fast cars. He qualified instead as an equipment officer, with the role of helping make sure that the dizzying array of kit needed for air force squadrons to operate was inventoried, accounted for and dispatched to the proper place.

And at least his desk wasn't in some dreary Ministry of Defence office in London. He was sent to Germany: to a base called RAF Bruggen, which was on the front line of the new, cold war with the Soviet Union.

John used the months before his call-up well. On leaving school, he went to work on Uncle Noel's farm in Cambridgeshire, this time with the benefit of not just driving a tractor but getting paid for it. He did have time for play as well. Noel's real nephew, Michael, was also working on the farm, and the two of them spent more than a few evenings in nearby pubs, drinking, flirting with girls and, on occasion, dancing with them. Still, to an extraordinary degree, he kept his focus riveted on what he – if, at this stage, no one else – viewed as his budding 'business'. Weeks before graduation, he'd formally set up a company. He called it Modern Enterprise Distributors and listed himself and his brother David as partners. With a mix of innate public-relations sense, raw optimism and infectious charm, he'd even secured its 'headquarters'. The company address was listed as 11 Old Bond Street, in the heart of old-money London. He'd managed to convince a middle-aged woman in one of the flats there to let him use her address. Not only that: she agreed that once he actually had titles to sell, he could bring them to the apartment. When orders arrived, she would post out the books and send the cash or cheques on to him.

His next step was to create something beyond his Austin Special pamphlet to sell. He settled on a pair of boxy, four-door, pre-war sedans – the Ford Eight and the Ford Ten – which British motor enthusiasts had begun refitting and souping up. John lacked the resources – or the time, with national service fast approaching – to get his hands on one of them. But having built the Austin Special, he figured it couldn't be all that difficult to do the same thing with the Fords. He culled all the available information from his car magazines, from owner's manuals and from visits to local garages. Within a matter of a months, he produced not just one but two books: *Building a Ford Ten Special* and the more comprehensive *Ford Special Builders Manual*, a 112-page volume complete with photos and several dozen of his illustrations, covering the Ford Eight as well.

Neither, however, was published under his own name. The ostensible author was one G.B. Wake. John decided to use a pseudonym, not because he knew he'd soon be in uniform; it was part of his growing sense of himself as a budding publisher, not just a pamphleteer, and of his business as not just a one-man show, but a *real* publishing house with a stable of expert authors. Nothing better conveyed his self-confidence, ambition and simple verve than the publicity material he drew up for the Ford builders' manual. It was, he said, aimed at, 'anyone contemplating building a Ford 8 or 10 special. It shows clearly and in detail how, for as little as £150, the impecunious motor enthusiast can build his own sports car, equal in performance, road handling, and beauty of line to a production car costing perhaps six times that figure.' He added that it was packed with, 'facts and figures, diagrams and photographs, on how a heavy saloon car can be completely transformed into a fast, good-looking sports car or a scintillating Gran Turismo saloon.'

Yet he reserved his most effusive prose for the book's 'author', and his words are especially revealing because they provide a window into how he saw himself as he was about to turn eighteen, and how he hoped that others would see him. 'G.B. Wake' was described as 'an experienced special builder of enormous enthusiasm' – a phrase that had the virtue, at least, of being *half*-true. He went on: 'The care and thoroughness with which he tackles any job are no more clearly illustrated than in the photographs in this book of his own specials. Not only has he given his own invaluable advice on the many aspects of special building, but also he has been able to draw on the specialised knowledge of firms and individuals, who have given him information that, otherwise, could not possibly have been obtained.'

The question now was how, or whether, he would manage to keep all of this going while serving Her Majesty's air force on a remote base in Germany.

Officially, it was called RAF Bruggen, a nod to the nearest town that was large enough to have a railway depot. But the locals called it *Flugpladt Elmt*, because the only civilian settlement in the immediate vicinity was, in fact, the tiny village of Elmt. A more accurate description might have been 'RAF in the Middle of Nowhere'. It was an amalgam of runways, concrete bunkers, offices and one-storey barrack blocks that had been carved out of a dense forest right on the the border with the Netherlands.

While it's hard for many people to imagine six decades later, it was also an installation with a vital military purpose. It had been completed just four years earlier. It was part of NATO's move to expand its forces in Europe in order to contain the Soviet Union. We know now that the Cold War did not erupt into hot war. Yet at the time, there was a real concern – a real *fear* – that the Soviets might use Warsaw Pact satellite countries like Poland, Czechoslovakia and East Germany as jumping-off points for an armoured advance into western Europe. There were even fall-back plans in case they did attack. RAF pilots who were in Bruggen at the same time as John can still remember hearing about one especially sobering contingency: a plan for the Dutch city of Nijmegen, on the River Waal just across the border, to dam up the river with enormous chunks of concrete, in the hopes of slowing down a Soviet advance by flooding the entire West German plain – including, of course, the RAF base. Still, the point of the British base was to help *prevent* such a Soviet attack. Shortly before John got there, its original fighter-jet units had been moved or disbanded. In their place was a pair of squadrons equipped with Canberras – state-of-the-art, high-altitude, jet-powered bombers. One squadron was earmarked for reconnaissance missions; the other, carrying small nuclear bombs, for attacks on targets in East Germany, Poland or Czechoslovakia if that proved necessary.

But remarkably, as John discovered when he arrived there in mid-1957, day-to-day life on RAF Bruggen had a lot less in common with grisly war classics like Spielberg's *Saving Private Ryan* than with Robert Altman's *M\*A\*S\*H*. The Canberra fighter crews never forgot the reason they were there. It could hardly have been otherwise: they were always required to be ready to take off within five minutes if they got the order. But there was an underlying sense of comradeship and, yes, fun – above all, but by no means only, on weekends. The installation also had the feel of a village in some ways. There were shops for household essentials, schools for the benefit of older officers with families, even a golf course. And, to John's particular delight, there was also a large complement of automobile enthusiasts.

It was a bit like Sutton Valence without adult supervision, and he adapted quickly. He was now not just older but more self-confident, and more certain about what he wanted to do with his life. He experienced none of the early jitters he'd had to deal with at boarding school. In fact, he would end up choosing to spend more than his required two years there, leaving only in 1960.

He had no trouble handling his desk job, in the base's General Equipment Park, especially once he discovered the wonders of something called Form 21-A. Only days after starting, he happened upon a discrepancy in the inventory – one of the dozens that inevitably crept in when managing a supply operation as large as RAF Bruggen's. Yet it wasn't just a few pairs of boots, some goggles, or an office hole-punch that appeared to be missing; it was one of the pre-fabricated wooden aircraft hangars used to shield aircraft from the elements, or from prying eyes. The problem was almost certainly down to a simple bookkeeping error. But since each hangar cost well over £1,000, the equivalent of around £20,000 today, it was sure to raise a stink somewhere in the bowels of the military bureaucracy back home. At a loss over what to do, John asked one of the warrant officers, who smiled indulgently and assured him there was nothing to worry about. 'You don't know about the 21-A?' he asked. It turned out to be a 'redesignation' form. All John had to do was to put the mix-up down to a typographical error, which he promptly did. What was now marked as missing wasn't a wooden *hangar*. It was a wooden *hanger*, the kind you draped your coat on.

Yet it was the people, not his job, that energised and enthused John during his nearly three years on the air base. As at Sutton Valence, he developed an early personal connection with one of the older, established officers: his superior, Squadron Leader Charles Lucas. But he soon also made other friends as well, beginning with Lucas's own effervescent nineteen-year-old daughter, Judi. In theory, at least, there was a work-related connection between the two of them. In addition to dealing with supply issues, the equipment park had a further function. It was in charge of a hundred-or-so German-made Magirus trucks which, if the Soviet tanks did rumble across the border, were detailed to evacuate all dependents on the base and drive them across Holland and France to Calais on the English Channel. Along with every wife or child old enough to have a licence, Judi was one of the designated drivers. While she never became John's girlfriend, the two of them hit it off from the start. And it was through Judi that he became an all-in participant in the camp's lively social life – breaching the usual

RAF divide between those who sat behind desks and the 'true' airmen who sat behind the controls of an aeroplane.

Judi's eventual husband, a twenty-one-year-old reconnaissance pilot named Hugh Mayes, became a close friend. He was then Judi's boyfriend – or, more accurately, one of several, since she deftly dated a handful of other young pilots and navigators as well, so that if one or another was on night patrol, she'd always have an enthusiastic escort in reserve. John became a familiar presence at the reconnaissance squadron's frequent, and not-infrequently raucous, off-duty parties. With Hugh, Judi and a rotating cast of others, he also ventured off the base to an assortment of bars and clubs in nearby towns like Munchengladbach, or further afield, in Cologne or Dusseldorf.

In one way, however, John was different from many of the other young officers. Most tended to date young women on the base, who were either the daughters of serving officers or worked in support roles. John did briefly go out with several of them, but he was soon drawn to a young German woman named Marianne Vissers. She was a bright, vivacious blonde, a year older than he was, whom he met on one of his nights out in Munchengladbach. The relationship was serious, on both sides, and not only because they partied together, laughed together, and began spending as much free time as they could find together; it was also because one of the qualities in John that attracted Marianne – something which at first puzzled her, then intrigued her and finally fascinated her – was his *other* love interest: cars, and the business that he was intent on building, piece by piece, around them.

It was in Bruggen where the business began to grow up. It was also where the pattern that would come to define his life during its early years – work hard, but play hard too – took root. John's stint on the RAF base was not just productive. It was enjoyable. He conveyed a bit of this in intermittent letters back to his parents on the tea plantation. But David, who had now also graduated from Sutton Valence, had a more direct sense of how things were going. Every couple of months, John would spend a few days back in England, and the brothers would almost invariably get together. The impact became clear as David began to map out his own future. After boarding school, he had at first contemplated going to university. But he needed to make up ground in maths before going that route. While looking at options for the relevant tutoring, he spent his first winter after graduation working as a Christmas sales assistant at the luxury London store Harrods, which promptly invited him to stay on and join its management-training programme. But David was certain he'd find little personal fulfilment from a life in retail sales, even at Harrods. So the next spring – even though national service had now ended – he enlisted in the RAF. Why? As he would recall years later: 'I figured John was having such a good time that I ought to give it a try.'

But the real fun for John at Bruggen involved cars: driving them, putting them through their paces, and, on at least one memorable occasion, crashing them. Among the fringe-benefits of being a British officer posted overseas was that he was exempt from automobile-purchase tax. It was a perk he deployed, on one of his early trips back to England, to buy a sleek, red MGA convertible. It became the first of what Hugh Mayes fondly remembers as 'John's passion wagons'. It was also the car that he crashed. The accident wasn't his fault. He was taking it for a spin on one of the back roads outside the camp. It was autumn, and there were tall rows of corn on either side of the narrow lane. He was testing the limits of the roadster when another driver overtook a car coming in the opposite direction and – because of the cornstalks, and the MG's low profile – didn't see John's car at all. The impact hurled it off the road and into the cornfield. John, amazingly, emerged unscathed. The MG didn't: it took months to make it whole, and drivable, again. Still, far from deterring him, that simply led to the purchase of Passion Wagon Number Two: a jet-black Jaguar Mark VII luxury saloon.

His cars were not just for nights out. The automobile enthusiasts on the base, Hugh Mayes prominent among them, had set up a motoring club dubbed the Bruggen Burners. Almost every weekend, they took their vehicles on high-speed 'road tests' on the runways. They also held 'navigation rallies' to explore the surrounding countryside. Though most of the nearby roads were farm-country lanes, Germany's Marshall Fund millions from the US were being deployed in a major national road-building programme. Since the new roads had yet to appear on local maps, reading the newly erected road signs was where the 'navigation' often came in. It proved an inexact science, especially since none of the Burners had anything approaching fluency in German. For months on end, John and Hugh were puzzled in particular by a series of signs, sometimes many miles apart, that pointed to a town that neither of them had heard of: *Umleitung*. A delighted Marianne finally resolved the mystery: *umleitung* meant 'diversion'.

Yet John worked hard, too: more than competently at his desk job, but passionately, and sometimes well past midnight, on what he was now describing to friends as his 'publishing company'. During his first few months, the focus was on merely keeping the business going, by selling more of the Austin and Ford Special booklets. Before leaving for Germany, he'd decided to supplement the arrangement with his Bond Street 'distributor' in order to provide for the possibility of handling larger quantities of books in future. Spotting an advert in *Exchange & Mart* placed by a Cambridge man who wanted to rent out his garage, John not only rented it as a place to store the books, but arranged for him to fill orders on commission. He grandly rechristened the garage as the Sporting Motorists Bookshop.

If he was going to sell more books, however, he also had to print more of them. He had carted an old Gestetner mimeograph machine with him from England, the same model he'd used at Sutton Valence for his first Austin pamphlet. Almost as soon as he got to Bruggen, he began churning out as many copies as he could. Hugh Mayes remembers more than once returning to his officer's mess room, only fifty yards or so from John's, and, as he tried to get to sleep, hearing the *kerchunk, kerchunk, kerchunk* as John turned the Gestetner handle and ran off page after page until the small hours of the morning. At least once every few months, he would collect the finished products and, removing the spare wheel and the passenger seat from the MGA, ferry them back to his 'book store' in Cambridge. One good thing, at least, about wrecking the MG was that the stately Jaguar could carry a lot more books.

Yet it was through Marianne that he took his first step toward becoming a *real* publisher. The idea was born near the end of his first year in Bruggen. Marianne was standing at his side amid the rhythmic clump of the Gestetner, when she suggested that maybe it might be easier to find a *professional* to produce the books instead. John had thought of that, of course, but had dismissed it as surely too expensive.

A few days later, however, Marianne took him along to one of several nearby printers who, in Germany's still war-affected economy, were eager for the work. She acted as both translator and co-negotiator, and within fifteen minutes the deal was done. It ended up *saving* money, not to mention a lot of elbow pain, over the humble mimeograph. When she and John collected the first batch of the Austin Special books a few weeks later, he turned to her and kept repeating, with growing wonder: 'It's proper printing. It's *proper* printing.'

He also saw it as an important milestone in creating a *proper* business, and in becoming a proper businessman – which was very much the persona he wore when he and Marianne travelled back to England in the winter of 1959. After delivering the latest consignment of books to the Cambridge garage, they headed north-west to visit David, who was a few months into his first air force posting at a maintenance and training base called RAF Cosford, a couple of dozen miles past Birmingham in the Midlands. It was late December, and David had invited them to join him and his comrades at their Christmas ball in the officers' mess hall. At the end of the evening, John led David outside and, smiling proudly, swept a majestic arm in the direction of the Jaguar Mark VII. 'Go on,' he said. 'Why don't you take it, and drive it to work tomorrow morning?' Gratefully accepting, David took the keys.

The following morning, he started it up and headed for his office. It was across the main road in the secure part of the base, guarded by sentries beside an imposing pair of recently installed wrought-iron gates. Though he had never driven any vehicle anywhere near as big as the Jaguar, it handled well, even with the film of ice on the road. But as he approached the entrance to the main base, he gently pumped the brakes, slowly turned the wheel, and sat helplessly as the back end slid outward and the car ploughed into the gates. The car was still drivable. But he could hear the tyres grate against the dented front wing as he manoeuvred the car past the startled sentries and into the base. He managed to get someone in the maintenance unit to pry the bumper loose, but it was obviously going to need further work to put it back into anything like its original condition.

Still, John was utterly unfazed as he took possession of it that afternoon and began the trip back to Germany, and he never mentioned it again. This was in part because John was almost never given to fits of temper, and certainly not towards his younger brother. But his response, or lack of it, was also in keeping with his sense of himself as John Haynes, successful businessman – for whom such a minor accident was really not worth fretting about.

It was *this* John Haynes, the businessman John Haynes, who increasingly came to the fore during his final months in Bruggen.

Not only did he churn out a steady stream of additional copies of his existing titles – all three of them. He added a fourth, this time with a *genuine* outside author. He was a thirty-five-year-old *Daily Mirror* journalist who was also an automobile enthusiast. His name was Allan Staniforth, and within a decade he would become something of a motoring legend, by designing and building a small, one-seater hill-climbing car dubbed the Terrapin. But now, Staniforth's preoccupation was to wed a sleek fibreglass Rochdale body shell with a common-garden, budget Ford known as the Popular. It resulted in what became known as the Rochdale GT. With a keen sense of trying to build on the Austin and Ford 'special' books he'd already published, John marketed Staniforth's account of how it was done under the title *Building a Gran Turismo Special*. As he got ready to return to England in early 1960, he was confident that this latest 'special' book would be just the beginning.

Yet for the first time since boarding school – in fact, for the first time in his life – he was about to discover that making his way in the world was a lot more daunting than he'd come to believe.

*Chapter Four*

# BUMPY LANDING

John Haynes left the RAF not with a plan, but with something more like an aspiration, a vision of his future self, and even that was still in soft focus. If you'd asked him at the time, he would have said: 'I am going to be a motoring publisher. A *successful* publisher. A successful *London* publisher.' And, on the heels of his nearly three years in Bruggen, he would have added: 'I'm going to have fun doing it.'

He arrived in London at the start of the sixties, the city's most vibrant decade since the Second World War, and he hit the ground running. He promptly found accommodation: first renting a roomy if slightly time-worn flat in Norfolk Crescent, off the Edgware Road, not far from Paddington Station; then a smaller but nicer bedsit in a detached house in Cranley Gardens, South Kensington. He found a one-room office, too, or more accurately *half* of a one-room office. He shared it with a marine outfitting business, and it was decorated to look like the inside of a boat. But its address was even more worthy of a 'successful London publisher' than the ostensible Bond Street 'headquarters', which it now supplanted. It was on Regent Street. And just weeks after his arrival, he formally registered a new business: J.H. Haynes & Co. Its trading name was Technical Books, and it had the grand total of one author on its list: 'G.B. Wake'.

John's working life didn't change much at first. In addition to his stately Jaguar, which he proudly drove around town, and his beloved MGA, which was mostly garaged at first, he purchased an old Mini van that was perfect for cramming with cartons of books. Once every six weeks or so, he would travel back to Germany, where all of his titles, including the old Austin Seven books, were still being printed. He'd spend at least a few extra days there, seeing Marianne and his RAF friends, then pile the stock into the Mini and drive it back to his 'bookshop' garage in Cambridge.

For much of his first year in London, that arrangement seemed to work. As the months passed, however, a range of pressures and preoccupations built up. His Bruggen commute was wearing enough. But it was made more difficult by the fact that his long-distance relationship with Marianne was also eroding. Since he was now 'working hard and playing hard' back home, he'd begun dating a number of young London women as well. Still, the main source of strain came from within: the unanticipated difficulty he found in living on his own, in dealing with the *reality* of the independence and autonomy, which had seemed so alluring back at Bruggen. How much different could life in London be, he'd thought, than the freelance freedom he'd managed to carve out for himself as an RAF officer, or when he was at Sutton Valence? But it *was* different. During all of his twenty-two years – on the air base, at boarding school, or as a child in Ceylon – he had never had to cook for himself, clean for himself, truly provide for himself. Yes, he'd enjoyed great freedom. But it was always with a structure around him – family, school, the RAF – as a kind of backstop. He still valued the freedom, and he had lost none of his enthusiasm for building his business. But he missed that source of assurance, steadiness, stability.

And we know this not because of anything John said at the time; we know it because of what he *did*. In the autumn of

1960, barely six months after having left Bruggen to embrace the alluring possibilities of civilian life in London, he rejoined the Royal Air Force.

He re-enlisted with the advantages of a 'long-service' officer, and gradually transitioned onto a new career track. Rather than managing bits of equipment, his new field – 'air movements' – would involving managing the comings and goings of aircraft and their cargo. Still, his two years at RAF Church Fenton in the north of England bore a remarkable resemblance to his time in Bruggen. The base was not quite the British equivalent of 'RAF in the Middle of Nowhere', but it wasn't Regent Street either. It was near an old market town called Tadcaster, about a dozen miles from Leeds.

Any lingering doubt he might have had about returning to the RAF disappeared just a few months later, early in 1961, when he sustained the greatest setback so far to his embryonic publishing business. Early one winter morning, he got a phone call from Cambridge. His 'bookshop' garage, packed with nearly 3,000 of his books, had gone up in flames. Years later, he would say that he'd learned an important lesson as a result, and it is true that never again would he fail to take the rudimentary precaution of insuring his business assets. But it was a huge jolt at the time. The financial hit was not just the final spur to ending his print-and-commute arrangement with Marianne in Germany. He was reduced to buying another Gestetner machine and churning out copies of his books the old way.

Still, even in these suddenly choppier waters, he remained more determined than ever to make his business work. And over time, he was able to turn to a newly important source of support: his immediate family. Barely a month after John had left Bruggen, Harold Haynes finally retired. With Vi and their now-teenaged daughter, Mary, he boarded a boat in Colombo and headed back from Ceylon to England. Harold had spent well over a decade setting aside a modest nest-egg and planning for life back home. Before returning, he'd rented a cottage for the three of them in Devon for their first few months. He'd even bought a new car – a little Triumph Herald saloon – from a dealership in Coventry.

It had been nearly two years since John or David had seen the rest of their family, and the two brothers carefully choreographed the return. David, on his own RAF base in the Midlands, was not too far from Coventry, so he collected the Triumph and drove it down to John's flat in London. The next morning, they set off in convoy, with John leading the way in his Jaguar, to meet the boat in Southampton. After a dockside embrace, John motioned his mother and young sister into the Jaguar and packed the family luggage into the boot. With David and Harold following in the Herald, he set out due west toward the rental cottage, 130 miles away in the West Devon village of Exbourne. About halfway there, John pulled over, and they stopped for lunch in Yeovil, at an old brownstone pub and inn called The Manor.

For the next two years, they actually saw very little of one another. John and David did sometimes make the trip down to Exbourne, but rarely, and only once at the same time, for the family's first Christmas back home. After John re-enlisted, both brothers had their RAF work to deal with. And it was a long drive, especially for John, whose base was more than 300 miles away from Devon. Yet it wasn't just the air force, or even the need to keep his publishing business going after the garage fire, that made it hard for John to get away. It wasn't so much the work as the *play*. The dating. The pubbing. And, above all, a new claim on his time which began as a pastime but very soon became a passion. In Bruggen, he'd always enjoyed driving his cars, and at times driving fast. But he'd never raced them. When he got back to London, and especially once he had returned to the RAF, he began donning his flimsy-looking helmet and prescription eye-goggles and spending weekends testing his skill, nerve and speed against hundreds of other amateur racing enthusiasts at circuits around the country.

He began with his trusty MGA, but that didn't last long. It might have *looked* like a racing car. But it took him only one weekend – at Brands Hatch, in the Kent countryside south-east of London – to conclude that he'd never be able to make it drive like one. It was too heavy, and it lacked the punch to compensate. Years later, he'd still remember climbing into the circuit's second turn, the fabled hairpin known as Druids, and almost sliding off the track.

A few weeks later, he tried again, at Silverstone, the now-iconic circuit that had been set up on the grounds of a wartime RAF base. But as he pushed the MG to its limits on the straight, an Austin Healey drew up alongside him and – in John's words – 'just walked away from me'. His response, just like at Sutton Valence, was to build his own.

He didn't go to a scrap-metal yard this time, however. He bought the components, in kit form, and set about assembling a Lotus Seven racer. Fortuitously, his old Bruggen friend, Hugh Mayes, was now also back in England and on the weekend racing circuit as well, and he pitched in with major modifications on the iconic original design. Together, they modified the suspension and put on an entirely new front end. John was attentive, almost to the point of obsession, about every detail. He wanted to end up not just with a race-worthy Lotus, but one with a decided edge on the starting grid. He fitted the car with a custom, five-speed gearbox. And in place of the standard, narrow wheels, he went out and had new, wider rims and tyres made in the hopes of giving it extra stability, and extra speed. The result was, by some distance, both lighter and much quicker than the MG, which he now began using to tow the Lotus on a small trailer.

Even with the Lotus, he was never at the very top of the growing amateur racing fraternity. But he placed in a number of the races, and he even won a few. And he loved everything about it: the challenge, the flirting with danger, and, perhaps as much as anything, simply being a part of this freewheeling family of 1960s car fans, with their often bright, often charming, and almost invariably attractive girlfriends. By the summer of 1962, he was matching them race by race, and increasingly girlfriend by girlfriend. It wasn't quite a case of his having a girl for every race circuit, but it wasn't that far off.

But in other important ways, his life was about the change, starting with his *real* family. His parents and Mary had now spent nearly two years in Devon. At first, they'd lived in the cottage in Exbourne, but a few months later Harold moved them into a more modern bungalow a few miles away. Then, putting thousands of miles on the Triumph Herald, he began a systematic search for a place to buy. He knew that anything like the equivalent of his Ceylon tea-plantation quarters would be beyond his means. The aim, as he ventured further and further eastwards in his excursions, was to find a spacious, attractive family home that was as near to London as he could realistically afford. In the end, he settled on a handsome detached house, with three bedrooms and a nice garden, in Yeovil. It was at the top end of a street called St Michael's Avenue, fringed by farmland yet only a few miles from The Manor, the pub where John had taken them for lunch on their first day back in England.

Harold's choice offered something else too. At the foot of the narrow drive that ran alongside the house was a garage. Almost as soon as they'd moved in, John came up with an idea to put it to use. With Harold's puzzled but willing acquiescence, he made it the successor to his ill-fated Cambridge book depository. It became the new Motorists Bookshop. Like its predecessor, it was a bookshop only in name. Its function was to handle mail-order requests for John's – and G.B. Wake's – books, post out the merchandise, and hold the cheques between his son's visits home.

It was not just the happy coincidence of their new business arrangement that soon made these visits more frequent. John's life in the RAF was changing as well. Promoted to the rank of Flight Lieutenant, he was soon to be reassigned to a training base in South Cerney, Gloucestershire. In place of the rarely attempted 300-mile trek from his north-of-England base to Devon, his drive from his new base to Yeovil was barely a quarter of that.

Yet he was also on the verge of another change. It occurred just a few months before the move to his new RAF post. But it came off base, and out of uniform, on his way to one of his weekend race meetings, at Brands Hatch. And while he had no way of knowing this at the time, it would have a deeper, and more lasting, impact than anything in his entire life.

*Chapter Five*

# RACING TEAM

It was an unseasonably brisk morning in June 1962 when John Haynes snaked his bright-red MGA through the outer-London traffic. With his Lotus tied on the trailer behind, and a scarf wrapped rakishly around his neck, he weaved into the centre of the city, through Sloane Square, between the pricey boutiques of the King's Road and, a few blocks later, into Smith Street, one of the exclusive residential roads that run like brick-and-stucco ribs between Chelsea's premier shopping avenue and the River Thames.

Three strikingly attractive young women were waiting outside the three-storey corner house at Number 28 Smith Street. Two were sisters, Jill and Ann Rowson, and John knew them well. In fact, Ann, though she was now engaged to one of the officers he'd worked alongside in Bruggen, was a former girlfriend. But the third was about to meet him for the first time. She was trim, with thick dark hair and wide-set brown eyes, and she watched with a wry smile as John tried fruitlessly to park his unwieldy racing rig amid the luxury cars occupying every available place.

If not for the urging of the Rowson sisters, she would not have been there at all. Annette Coleman-Brown lived in the first-floor flat at Number 28, and had invited Jill, a work colleague, and then Ann in as roommates. She had a boyfriend at the time, a motorcycle enthusiast who lived not far from her parents in Worthing, on England's south coast, and she had been planning to go back there for the weekend. But she'd been tiring of the boyfriend for some time. 'You like motor racing, don't you?' Jill had asked her the night before. 'Why not stick around here? Our friend Johnny is coming down to race at Brands Hatch, and I'll introduce you.'

Annette was twenty-four years old, seven months younger than John. She was a free spirit: bright, adventurous, at ease with herself, armed with a self-confidence she had neither the need nor inclination to advertise. She was also a beautiful young woman: when she'd first come to London a couple of years earlier, she'd even briefly worked as a fashion model.

Her own family's back story was every bit as intricate as John's. When her parents married, it was not so much a May–September pairing, as a question of January and December.

Her father, British Army Major William Freeme Coleman, was 72 at the time. Her mother – Dilys, though known to friends and family as Dee – was only twenty-eight. Major Coleman's military career never took him quite as far as Ceylon, though he did serve in British-ruled India, Egypt and South Africa. But Annette never really knew him. By the time of the Second World War, he'd retired to a life of country pleasures in a large home near Devon, in the south-west of England. Just two months into the war, in November 1939, he was riding out to lead the local foxhunt and fell off of his horse. He died days later, shortly after Annette's first birthday.

Dee met the man whom Annette would always think of as her father, Raymond Brown, about a year later, by which time she had sold the family home and moved with her little daughter into a small cottage nearby. But the war years upended things for all of them. Ray was a home-front army captain, moving from base to base around England. Dee, not unreasonably, decided to decamp with her daughter to Bristol, where her parents lived.

But for nearly two years, beginning in early 1941, the extended family found itself shuttling between Bristol and Cardiff, in Wales, where Dee's father also owned a house, as German aircraft launched bombing raids on both cities. By 1943, the intensity of the air raids on Bristol had begun to slacken, and they settled back in there – an especially welcome respite for Dee, since Raymond was now stationed not far away. They married. They bought a small home near the south coast, in Bournemouth, where a second daughter, Penelope, was born in October 1943, and as the war drew to a close, Dee helped make ends meet by managing a series of little inns and hotels in the area.

A couple of years after the war, in 1947, with a sense of adventure that then-nine-year-old Annette would absorb and later emulate, Dee and Ray decided to strike out for pastures fresh.

The plan, initially, was to take the luxury America ocean liner, S.S. *Washington*, to New York City. And the four of them did indeed board the ship in Southampton. But during its stopover in the Irish port city of Cork, Dee and Raymond had second thoughts, and decided to get off there instead.

They bought a large Georgian mansion. It had seen better days, but it had ample grounds and a nice garden. Its perch on a hillside called Montenotte gave it a lovely view over the city and the River Lee below, and Dee, with her inn-management experience, set about turning it into one of the city's first truly European-standard hotels. Since a fair amount of renovation was required, the family's first few months were not easy. They stayed in a succession of decidedly *non*-European-standard hostelries. Even compared to post-war England, where rationing was still in effect, life in 1940s Cork could best be described as rudimentary. Their rooming-house dinners often boiled down, quite literally, to a choice between mutton and potatoes ... or potatoes and mutton.

But the Lee View Hotel opened in 1948 and Dee made a success of it. She was a natural hotelier: sociable, with a stylishness that at times bordered on flamboyance, and what Americans might call spunk. She was also something of a pistonhead. The Coleman-Browns' 'family' cars were without exception sporty. When Dee was younger she had even dabbled in racing, trying her luck in local hill-climb competitions. Since not just the hotel, but the city around it, began to flower during the 1950s, it was, all in all, an enjoyable, and happy, place for Annette to spend her early teenage years.

But that ended late in 1954, just after her sixteenth birthday, with a new, and decidedly directionless, family adventure. Piling into a newly purchased Hillman Minx family saloon, they drove back to Dee's parents' home in Bristol and then, after loading the car onto a channel ferry a few weeks later, across France, through northern Spain and finally to Majorca, where they would spend nearly half a year. Then, they retraced their footsteps. After a series of nomadic stays in the south and west of England, they ended up in north London, in a house near Alexandra Palace. It was to be a jumping-off point for Ray – or so her stepfather bravely hoped – to find a post as a stockbroker with one of the banks in the City of London. Sadly, bravery in itself did not prove a sufficient qualification for a banking job. A month or so later, the family decamped again, to Worthing, which would remain home for the remainder of Annette's parents' lives, and where Ray joined, and ultimately bought, an estate agency.

Annette's early working life was pretty nomadic as well. Before they left London, at around the time she turned seventeen, she had found a junior clerk's job in the Pearl Insurance Company in the City. The work was enjoyable enough. It was made even more so by the support of her boss, a hunting enthusiast who took her for shooting lessons at a nearby gun club. The result, though not likely to add much to her CV in the insurance world, was an undeniably impressive talent for firing a 22-calibre long rifle. When the family left for Worthing, she spent a few months helping Ray in the estate agency before looking around for other jobs. She briefly studied nursing at the local hospital, but then found a post as a bank clerk in nearby Hove – work that she quite liked, until deciding to join a friend on a fashion-modelling course. It was fun, she was good at it, and she was offered steady work. Around the time of her twenty-second birthday, she decided to set out to look for modelling work in London. That was not just brave, but brash: though the advent of the Twiggy era was still several years away, the modelling scene in early-1960s London was already becoming not merely competitive; it was almost Darwinian.

Soon convinced it was not for her, Annette spotted an advert in a London paper, placed by the Illinois-based international business consulting firm George S. May. 'Clerical staff,' it said. 'With modelling experience.' The translation, she would remember thinking at the time, was presumably: 'Tall, attractive, not too stupid.' Since she was qualified on all those counts – and *more* than qualified on the third one – she duly applied. The days that followed her interview were nerve-wracking. They'd made it clear they'd liked her, but said they'd be seeing a couple of other candidates and would get back in touch by the end of the week. By late Friday, Annette had heard nothing. So she phoned them, and was put through to none other than her future roommate, Jill Rowson, who was the personnel director's secretary. 'Thank goodness you called,' Jill said. 'I'd somehow lost your contact information. But yes, you have the job.'

The company's London office was near the Savoy Hotel on The Strand. It was the hub for the company's growing list of European clients, mostly at that time in Scandinavia. She was hired as a 'statistics clerk', collating and organising feedback from the various projects on the continent for broader analysis back home. It was interesting work. It paid well enough for her to rent a flat in Chelsea. And it left her with the freedom, not just to enjoy her life in the capital, but to make regular forays back to Worthing to see her family or, with increasing frequency, her motorcycling boyfriend.

But that relationship survived only a couple of weeks after her first Brands Hatch excursion with John Haynes. It was not just that she found him attractive, intriguing, and just plain fun, it was also abundantly clear to their friends – not least to Ann Rowson, who had some personal expertise in the area – that John was, if anything, more smitten by Annette.

Over the next couple of months, they spent every weekend at whatever race circuit John had chosen to race his Lotus. It was in the autumn of 1962, when they'd been going out for about three months, that she realised she was destined to be more than just the latest of his girlfriends. After all, as she'd remarked to Ann after their first meeting, the country seemed absolutely *littered* with them. He had invited her for the first time to join him for the weekend at the RAF base in Yorkshire, with a race scheduled not far away on the Saturday. They drove up from London together in the MGA. When they pulled to a stop outside the base, an undeniably lovely blonde girl, with the wonderfully unlikely name of Mandy Trollope, rushed forward. Arms extended, she shouted: 'Johnny! Johnny Haynes! Where have you been? I haven't seen you in months!' Uncommonly unsettled, John smiled, took her hands, and motioning toward Annette, said: 'Hi. Let me introduce you to my girlfriend ...'

His life wasn't all racing. Though with less single-minded focus since becoming a fixture on the amateur racing scene, John had by no means abandoned his hope of turning his motoring publications into a solid, sustainable business. He told Annette that he was sure that would play some part in his future. Yet especially at the beginning, by far most of

*above* Boy meets car: two-year-old John Haynes behind the wheel of his first racer, on the tea estate in Ceylon.

*right* Riding tandem: with his younger brother, David, in Ceylon.

*below* Child of empire: six-year-old John (second ) with his parents, brother David and staff members outside the estate tea factory in Ceylon.

**Top left and middle** *Road trip: snapshots of John's father with his younger sister, Mary; and his mother with the three children during a picnic excursion in the hill country of Ceylon.*

**Above** *Fancy dress: 11-year-old John kitted out as "William Brown", his early literary hero from the Just William books, flanked by Mary as Little Red Ridinghood and David, as a bus conductor.*

**Below left** *Valedictory smile: John proudly displaying an achievement award from his prep school in Ceylon, shortly before he and David left for boarding school in England.*

**Below** *Settling in: with his house master and housemates on a weekend picnic at Sutton Valence School, in Surrey.*

**Opposite top left** *Reunion: with his mother, Vi, a trip back from Ceylon to visit her two sons in Surrey*

**Opposite top right and bottom** *How it all began: John's first "Haynes Manual", and the Austin 750 Special he built at Sutton Valence from the skeletal remains he reclaimed from a local scrapyard*

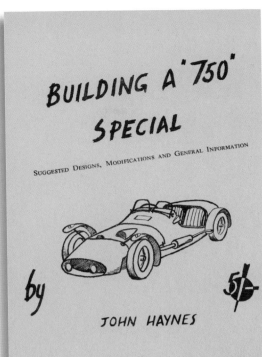

THIS PAGE *Artist in residence: some of the artworks that won John senior art prizes in his last three years at school.*

**OPPOSITE PAGE**

**Top** *Reconnaissance party: John (front row, fourth from right) with his circle of friends in the air force reconnaissance squadron at RAF Bruggen, near the German-Dutch border.*

**Middle** *Cheek to cheek: with Judi Lucas, the teenage daughter of his superior officer in the base's General Equipment Park and one of his closest friends during his years at RAF Bruggen.*

**Left bottom** *European union: Marianne Vissers, the young German woman he met while at RAF Bruggen. His first serious girlfriend, she also helped arrange professional printing for his handful of automotive books as he sought to build them into a publishing business.*

**Right** *Shoulder to shoulder: with Ann Rowson, John's girlfriend, and later the London flatmate and matchmaker who brought him together with his future wife, Annette.*

**Above** *Starting line: John behind the wheel of his MGA in the early stages of his weekend-racing years.*

**Below** *Gaining ground: overtaking on the outside.*

bove *Countdown: John in his Lotus on the starting grid at Goodwood, Sussex, just weeks before his and* **net**te's *wedding. Early in the race, he would end up spinning off the track while coming out of the chicane,* **t**ting *the bank on the side and getting thrown out onto his back.*

**elow** *Aftermath: the Lotus, after the accident at Goodwood.*

*Above Wedding bliss: John and Annette emerging from the church near Worthing where they were married, with his RAF friends forming a guard of honour.*

*Left Best of brothers: John with brother David, his best man.*

*Below Honeymoon: holidaying with Annette and friends in Spain after the wedding.*

their time was spent either at race tracks, or in getting to and from them.

Annette genuinely enjoyed racing. Having accompanied her Worthing boyfriend not just to motorbike competitions but car races as well, she was both a supportive and knowledgeable companion. She also came in handy in other ways.

At the end of December 1962, just months after they'd met, London was hit with its fiercest snowstorm in decades, part of what would become known as the 'big freeze', and deposit of drifts of two to three feet all across the south of England. When they woke up on the morning of 31 December, there was already half a foot of snow in London, and they were due at a New Year's Eve party that night more than 100 miles south-west, with John's parents' in Yeovil. Ordinarily, it would have been a pleasant three-hour drive. But it ended up taking nearly eight hours, as the snow streamed down and the drifts thickened. The MGA was not exactly ideal in such circumstances. Every ten minutes or so, John would find himself stuck in a snowdrift. Annette would leap out and push, almost invariably falling on her face in the process. Years later, John would tell her, perhaps only half-joking: '*That* is when I decided I was going to marry you.'

And it was only weeks afterwards that John did ask her to be his wife. By the spring of 1963, they began planning a late-June wedding: one year, almost to the day, since they'd met.

In truth, Annette's mother, Dee, did the lion's share of the planning, so there was little noticeable effect on John's racing schedule. He even entered a final, pre-marital race at Goodwood, in Sussex, at the end of May. John travelled from his base to the circuit on his own, but Annette arrived from London with one of his old RAF friends in ample time for the start. They posted themselves close to the finish line, assured of a good view each time John and the others came round onto the long straight that anchored the roughly two-mile track. The first sign of any trouble came on the third lap: John's Lotus simply didn't show. There was no announcement that anything had necessarily gone wrong. At Goodwood, at least back then, there was no announcement of anything. Annette, along with John's tall, burly air force mate, rushed across onto the infield. With the late-spring grass reaching almost to shoulder-level, it was like ploughing through incoming surf during a storm tide. Worse, they could see people converging in the distance on the opposite side of the circuit. So *something* had clearly happened.

By the time they reached John, he was in an ambulance. He had spun out on the right-hand corner after the chicane. The Lotus had hit the bank on the side of the track but had continued to roll, flipping him out of the car onto his back. He was clearly in great pain. But he was alive, something that would not have been anything near certain if he had been strapped in at the time of the crash. He opened his eyes, grimacing, saw Annette peering down at him, and managed a smile. She squeezed his hand, smiled back, and said: 'Don't think you're getting out of the marriage that way, John!'

By the time of their wedding – June 25, a pleasantly warm Tuesday afternoon on the south coast – he was surprisingly close to being his old self. He was still taking painkillers. His back remained stiff. He obviously wasn't going to be racing any time soon, if only because the Lotus was a comprehensive wreck. Yet with the ceremony set for a beautiful twelfth-century Norman church a few miles from Annette's family home in Worthing, John did drive down to Yeovil from the RAF base in Gloucestershire in the MGA, where he was joined by his parents, David and Mary for the drive to one of Worthing's fine old waterfront hotels, the Burlington.

All seemed as if it was going to plan until, less than an hour before the Haynes contingent was due to leave for the church, David realised than John was nowhere to be found. It seemed unlikely that he'd done a runner, but his brother was not entirely sure until, with minutes to spare, he suddenly reappeared. 'Been buying a wedding present,' he said, smiling. It was a used but functional IBM typewriter boasting 'proportional spacing', which would allow his new bride to produce professionally justified typescripts once he turned his mind back to his motoring books. John did have the good sense, at least, to withhold the present until they were back from their honeymoon.

John and his family were duly in place when Annette arrived at the church with her family in a Rolls-Royce. She beamed with unalloyed pleasure as he strode up the aisle beside her in his dress uniform and officer's cap, and both of them had a look of pure joy as they exited the church to an honour guard made up of four of John's fellow RAF comrades. After the couple's reception and wedding night at the Burlington, John drove them in the MGA to a Kent airfield. It had a small transport plane equipped to take cars across the channel to France, the starting point for a honeymoon that culminated on Spain's Costa Brava.

It was an adventure. It was fun. Both of these qualities were very much part of what had drawn John and Annette together. But as John's only slightly tongue-in-cheek IBM wedding gift made clear, he saw them as life partners not just in play, but in work. And he still saw his working future in finding a way to build a profitable company around writing, and publishing, books about cars.

That renewed focus didn't kick in immediately. But when it did – during the couple's next RAF posting, more than 3,500 miles from England – it would mark the first real step toward creating the Haynes motor-manual business.

*Chapter Six*

# THE BIG IDEA

If you were in the picture-postcard business, it would have been hard to imagine a more magical setting: on the rim of an ancient volcanic crater, gazing out across a vast expanse of perfectly sun-sparkled sea. The old Arab town, sloping down toward the shoreline, was actually called Crater, and it lay across a deep-water harbour from a little outcrop of land called Steamer Point.

Yet in the mid-1960s, when Flight Lieutenant John Haynes and Annette began their two-year assignment there, Aden – in what is now Yemen – was not a place from which you'd send postcards. After a century and a half as a way-station between Britain and its Asian and African colonies, it found itself at the centre of a final retreat from imperial power.

India, the jewel in Britain's Asian crown, had gained independence in 1947. Months later, British Mandatory rule in Palestine ended, with the establishment of the State of Israel. In the 1950s, the pro-British monarchy in Egypt was toppled. Its pan-Arabist President, Gamal Abdel Nasser, went on to nationalise the Suez Canal – a move Britain sought to reverse by force of arms in 1956, only to be ordered into a humiliating climbdown by the West's *new* superpower, the United States. And in December 1963, Kenya, Britain's prized colony on the east coast of Africa, became independent.

Still, the British retained significant military power, as well as strategic and economic interests in the areas where they had for so long ruled. And Aden, near the vast oil lands of Arabia at the gateway to the Red Sea, embodied their determination to retain a physical foothold as well. Just above the crowded alleyways of Crater, a few hundred yards up the coast, was a sprawling Royal Air Force installation. It was called Khormaksar. It was not just a strategic lynchpin for the Middle East. It was the transit hub for British military traffic to its remaining outposts in Asia, and Africa as well. With nearly 5,000 officers, enlisted men and staff; hundreds of fighter planes and bombers and helicopters; and hundreds more flights passing through each week, it was the largest single RAF base in the world.

And by the time John Haynes took up his post, it was also the most precarious. Two separate guerrilla groups – inspired by Nasser's militancy, and supported by the new Arab Republic of Yemen to the north – were determined to see the British leave once and for all. In December 1963, the larger of the two, the National Liberation Front, mounted a grenade attack on Britain's High Commissioner as he was arriving at Khormaksar for a flight back to London.

He survived, with a minor shrapnel injury to one of his hands. But a woman bystander was killed on the spot and the commissioner's political aide was seriously wounded and died a few days later. The attack led to the declaration of the so-called Aden Emergency, and a concerted British military fightback.

And almost exactly one year later, just after John arrived there in late 1964, the guerrillas attacked the RAF base once again. This time, they targeted a Christmas Party. A little girl was killed, and four other children were injured.

Annette was still in England when John left for Aden. She and John had spent the first few months of their marriage in a flat in Cirencester before moving to married quarters in his RAF base in Gloucestershire. On one score at least, their married life wasn't markedly different from before: John had resumed his motor racing. Though the Lotus was gone, he found a replacement that had excited him even more. He bought a wonderfully manoeuvrable, fibreglass-bodied Elva Courier, to which he added extra power by fitting an 1800cc MGB engine.

From the outset, it was clear that Annette had neither the desire, nor intention, to be merely a stay-at-home wife. That was fortunate. John, of course, was equally enthusiastic about her working, and ultimately about their forging a working *partnership*. At first, she did typing for a group of solicitors down the stairs from their apartment. But she soon began spending much of her time deploying her wedding gift – the IBM typewriter – on the latest of John's book projects.

It would be the first to display a Haynes logo on its cover. It also marked a return from the humble mimeograph to 'proper' printing. And that was thanks to John's brother, David. He finished his own RAF stint in the summer of 1964. During his final stretch in uniform, he'd befriended a grounded pilot who was working in the printing department, and he learned the basics of the trade. Upon leaving the air force, he briefly moved in with Harold, Vi and Mary in Yeovil. But he soon invested in an offset-litho press and set himself up as a contract printer in a slightly ramshackle, mid-terrace house in the centre of town, a mile or so away.

The new Haynes book covered the humble Ford Anglia, and for Annette, it proved to be hard work. It was true that the IBM made it possible to produce fully justified, print-ready text. But it was a torturously tedious process. It meant doing every single page twice. First, you had to type it normally. Then, using the longest line, you'd mark a right-hand margin in pencil and manually calibrate how much spacing to add to each of the other lines to make them match. Yet she got the job done. John promoted the finished product as a 'workshop manual'. But it was laid out in standard book format. It had photos, but it lacked detailed drawings. It looked more like a library reference than a practical manual for a car-owner. To John's disappointment, especially since he was about to head off to the Middle East, it also sold very few copies.

Still, once he arrived in Aden, and especially when Annette joined him early in 1965, there was little time to fret about that. Khormaksar was not only much larger than RAF Bruggen. Crucially, it wasn't living with the *fear* of war, but its reality. True, there were no nuclear weapons to worry about, nor the prospect of hundreds of Soviet tanks poised to rumble forward. But as the ambush on the Christmas party at the airbase had made chillingly clear, both the NLF and its rival guerrilla movement – the Front for the Liberation of Occupied South Yemen – were determined to drive out the British by force.

There were two principal 'fronts' in the battle between the insurgents and the British armed forces. One lay literally just outside the perimeter fence of Khormaksar: the densely packed streets of Crater, where both the NLF and FLOSY had supporters, stocks of grenades, makeshift explosive devices and small arms. Much of the weaponry had been smuggled in from the other front: the mountainous region of Radfan, to the north of Aden near the border with the Yemen Arab Republic. Khormaksar itself was not under immediate threat. After the Christmas attack, security precautions on the base, already tight, had been ratcheted up further. Crater was obviously a no-go area for off-duty officers or troops. But a more general night-time curfew was soon imposed on all personnel, including those, like John and Annette, who lived in one of the string of apartment blocks for British personnel outside the confines of the base.

John's job in Bruggen had been to manage, and occasionally fiddle, RAF inventories. Now, he was a senior officer in Khormaksar's air movements squadron, with a core operational role: co-ordinating and handling the many hundreds of aircraft each month that ferried in passengers, supplies and other freight. Although there was a civilian air terminal at the opposite end of the runway, in view of the security situation, the RAF was also tasked with processing BOAC and civilian charter flights – as well as medical-evacuation flights from the fighting in Radfan. They worked on a shift rota: 12 hours or more at a stretch, depending on events and the weight of traffic, then a couple of days off to decompress before going back on duty.

As so often happens in war zones, the pressure, and potential dangers, created an extraordinary closeness, not just among the officers, but with those who served under them. There was also an outsized appetite for shared enjoyment during off-duty hours. The base itself had a network of clubs that showed films, served drinks and meals, and held parties and dances.

And even with the curfew regulations, Steamer Point, about a mile away, offered all that and more. Its name came from its initial imperial role: as a coaling, and later a refuelling station for sea traffic from India and other Asian colonies returning, through the Red Sea and the Suez Canal, to England. During the 1960s insurgency, it remained a docking station for British navy vessels, and BP still ran an oil refinery there. So the area was well protected. It offered a choice of restaurants where meals could be enjoyed in the pleasant night-time air during the winter and spring months. Summer in Aden, however, was stultifyingly hot. Temperatures hovered around 40 degrees Celsius, and when the sultry *khamsin* sandstorms blew in from the desert, it could be dusty as well. All the more reason to be thankful for access to the nearby beach, which was fenced in and regularly patrolled.

There was no motor racing, and to John's lasting regret, he had sold the Elva Courier before heading out from England. But he and Annette were fully fledged participants – indeed, leading lights – in the rest of Khormaksar's social life. Some of it happened at home: along the line of five-storey apartment buildings than ran alongside Ma'alla, the ruler-straight road between Khormaksar and Steamer Point, John, Annette and their RAF friends would often gather in one of their flats for drinks, and sometimes dancing. Under the tightened security regulations, however, one of them would always have to be on armed duty downstairs in case of trouble. Technically, they also had to wrap up by curfew, at midnight. In fact, the parties almost always went on past midnight, at which point the revellers would gather on the roof to check the position of the British Army Land Rovers on their security rounds. When there was a gap, the guests would rush downstairs and, literally ducking from pillar to pillar, doorway to doorway, make their way back home.

At more formal events on the air base, with Annette in a sleek evening dress at his side, John would show up in a neatly tailored mess dress uniform, ebullient and smiling and dapper. There was at least a dollop of vanity in his bearing, though it was leavened by his own ability to laugh at it. He did know that he cut a rakish figure, and he enjoyed it. Nowhere was this more evident than in his choice of eyewear. He needed prescription glasses, and it would be some years before contact lenses became a practical alternative. So, in early-rock-star mode, he always wore prescription *sunglasses*, day or night.

And it was the sunglasses that ended up getting him into trouble.

The problem began during one of his night shifts. John was on the runway at Khormaksar, going through formalities with the pilot of a charter aircraft that had just landed. From across the tarmac came the unmistakable voice of Group Captain Michael Beetham, the Second World War veteran who had been installed, just a week before John's arrival, as base commander. With far more aircraft and personnel than Khormaksar had been designed to accommodate, and the intensifying conflict with the insurgents, Beetham was an obvious choice. A decade later, he would become overall commander of the Royal Air Force, and he was an old-school officer: serious, laser-focused, and uncompromising on matters of organisation and discipline. At Khormaksar, he quickly became known – only behind his back – as The Bastard Beetham. 'Haynes!' he bellowed. 'Why are you wearing sunglasses at midnight?'

'So I can see, sir,' he replied. It was not meant to be insubordinate – merely to explain that they were corrective lenses – but to Beetham, it sure sounded that way. 'Nonsense,' he snapped. 'Don't let me catch you wearing them again.' The reprieve lasted exactly seven days. John, sunglasses intact, was processing another incoming flight when Beetham strode out and said, not unreasonably: 'I thought I told you not to wear those.' John apologised. But a couple of days later, he received a formal order: he and Annette were being transferred out of Khormaksar, for a three-month tour to RAF Eastleigh, just outside Nairobi in Kenya.

As punishments went, it wasn't exactly onerous. One of the junior officers working under John – a pilot officer named David Hyland with whom John and Annette had become friends – remembers the response in the rest of the unit to the news of John's sudden forced departure: 'We were all trying to work out what *we* had to do wrong to get sent to Kenya!'

The official name of the Nairobi base had in fact been changed. It was no longer RAF Eastleigh, but *KAF* Eastleigh, since it was home to the embryonic air force of an independent Kenya. But a continued British presence was accepted as in everyone's interest, not least because Britain was supplying and training the new KAF. There also remained a large British civilian population, both in Nairobi and in the countryside, with a lifestyle that had familiar echoes of John's planter-family childhood in Ceylon. Annette would later recall their months in Kenya as 'absolutely wonderful'. John's main job turned out to be to go shopping: in the lush, open-air market in the centre of Nairobi. Then, in what arguably still qualified as an 'air movement' role, he would arrange to fly a mouth-watering assortment of fresh fruit and vegetables back to Aden, providing the commanding officers with an alternative to the usual fare of tinned products.

Group Captain Beetham's exile of John Haynes thus appears to have worked out well for both parties. And something of a truce resulted. If Beetham did notice John's dark glasses once he returned, he seems to have decided they were not worth further comment.

Still, Haynes's time in Aden was not entirely without further incident. One, in particular, dramatised qualities that would mark his future life in business: a self-confidence sometimes bordering on bravado, a sense of deep indignation when he felt that he or others whom he cared about had been wronged, and a deep sense of loyalty to those who worked with or for him.

This time, the lead character in the drama was not Beetham, but the AOC – the commanding officer – of RAF forces in Aden. He was a figure with an even more towering reputation than Beetham. His name was James Edgar Johnson, though he was universally known as Johnnie Johnson. He had been one of Britain's ace fighter pilots during the Second World War, having downed some three dozen German aircraft. He was daring, debonair, and damned if he was going to suffer fools: specifically British Army fools. Having heard one too many complaints from army officers when he'd theatrically tip a wing or swoop low over trees or buildings when landing, he had issued an iron edict: there would be no army personnel on any aircraft when he was at the controls.

The run-in with Johnson did not involve John, but his second in command, a flying officer named David Welsh with whom both he and Annette had become close friends.

One night when Welsh was on duty – aware that Johnson was planning to fly to Kenya the following morning for one of his occasional golf outings – an army brigadier walked into the office and calmly declared that he'd just been at a cocktail party with Johnson. 'Johnnie said I could go down with him for a game of golf tomorrow, so I just wanted to let you know so you can put me on the flight.'

Welsh actually knew the brigadier – Welsh's own father had served under him a few years back in Germany – but also knew trouble when he saw it.

'I'm sorry, sir,' he said. 'The flight's fully booked.'

The brigadier wasn't buying that. He knew how things worked, he said. There was always space on such flights. 'Just put me somewhere up front.' Welsh said no, politely but unwaveringly, three more times before the brigadier pulled rank. 'I'm going to give you an order,' he said. 'Put me on the flight.' And so Welsh did.

It took only minutes after take-off the next morning for things to blow up. Even before Welsh realised that Johnson was turning back, Beetham pulled up in his Land Rover. He came straight to Welsh. 'Did you put that army officer on the flight?' he asked. When Welsh said, yessir, Beetham said: 'Well, Johnny's coming back. I think you might want to meet him … Or perhaps you might *not* want to.'

When the plane pulled to a stop and the front hatch opened, Johnson started down the ladder and yelled: 'Who's the stupid bugger who put that army officer on my flight?'

'I did, sir,' Welsh said.

Johnson removed his helmet and, in one perfect motion, hurled it at Welsh, striking him square on the forehead and knocking him over, with blood seeping from the wound. 'Johnson's aim probably saved me from being exiled to Alaska,' he'd recall years later. 'Because he had hit me, he really couldn't do anything more.'

But John Haynes could.

When he returned to duty the following day, he told Welsh: 'We're going to get that army brigadier.'

The brigadier was flying off to London that day and had been unable to reclaim his suitcase from Johnnie Johnson's flight quickly enough to take it with him. On his return a couple of weeks later, assuming that the air-movements team would have taken care of it, he came in to reclaim his baggage. On the first point, he was right; Haynes himself had gone into the hold and got the brigadier's case, but he'd told Welsh to keep it in his flat for a while.

'We've sent signals everywhere to locate it, sir,' Welsh replied to the brigadier. 'We just can't imagine what happened. But we'll find it, don't worry.'

When he returned a week later, to be told there'd still been no luck, he tried without much success to hide his mounting sense of panic. 'Look,' he said, 'I had top-secret documents in my baggage. That's a court-martial offence. And there's a documents-audit next week. I wonder if you could help me find the baggage.'

'We'll do our best, sir,' Welsh replied.

'We'll wait until the very last day,' Haynes said, smiling, when he'd left.

That is what they did, in fact holding off until the late afternoon of the final day, before contacting him.

'The brigadier knew what we'd done, I'm sure,' Welsh recalls, 'but he'd been punished. And ultimately, it was down to John's loyalty, his feeling that I'd been put in an impossible position by this officer. It was a kind of kinship he established.'

Not all of their brushes with higher authority were so fraught. With Britain's future hold on Aden increasingly at issue, a number of top-level military and political figures flew in to Khormaksar on Haynes' watch. Just before he began his posting,

Britain's 1964 general election had replaced the Conservatives with a Labour Party government. Harold Wilson was Prime Minister. And his defence secretary – the outspokenly anti-colonialist Dennis Healey – flew out to Aden in the spring of 1965. Barely an hour before the plane touched down, the phone rang, and an officer said that the AOC – Johnnie Johnson – wanted the steps that would be wheeled up the plane to be given a fresh coat of paint. Air Force blue, Haynes was told. He started to explain the obvious potential problem: there was no way the paint would be dry by the time Healey's plane touched down. But the officer had already hung up, so he got it done.

Healey had many engaging qualities. He was smart, he was cheerful, he was down to earth. And he was also reputed to enjoy his gin and tonic. Haynes himself made a point of joining the group that climbed the stairs to meet him, so that he could warn the defence secretary not to touch the handrails on the way down. 'I'm afraid they're wet, sir,' he said. But whatever libation Healey had taken on the ten-hour flight made the point moot. Steadying himself on the way down the steps, he duly shook hands with the VIP greeting party awaiting on the ground, more than a few with pristine white gloves and all of them ending up with a sticky, Air Force-blue souvenir memento of their encounter with the Defence Secretary. John was blamed, of course. But perhaps because the order had come from on high, his first foray into painting since his art classes at Sutton Valence was soon forgotten.

He also managed to avoid sanction for another, ostensibly more serious flouting of RAF practice during his final year in Aden. It was classic John, combining qualities that had first flourished in boarding school and would remain throughout his business life: an instinctive attraction for any new, untapped business opportunity, allied with a determination, optimism and devil-may-care confidence that allowed him to convince not just himself, but others, that his scheme might actually succeed.

The idea had first been put to him by another officer, who had been organising it before heading home at the end of his tour, and it took on ever greater appeal for John during the metronomic shifts spent handling the growing number of aircraft in and out of Khormaksar. A lot of the traffic involved military transports. But his unit was also responsible for civilian flights – not just BOAC ones, but a good number operated by the Scottish charter airline Caledonian – which was used by the air force for transporting military personnel and their families. As he and Annette were planning a two-week trip to England in the early autumn of 1966, John realised that dozens of others on the base would like to be doing the same thing during the summer. So he figured he'd talk to the people at Caledonian, whom he knew well by now, and lease one of their planes for return trips (costing half the price of a BOAC flight).

It wasn't really about the money. As David Hyland remembers it, the seats on the initial flight were sold off at barely above cost, the only benefit being that John and Annette in effect got their places free. Overhead costs came to a sum total of zero, because off-duty personnel willingly handled the take-off and landing arrangements. But the demand for such a service was obvious, and within a month or so, John and another senior officer, named Mike Barham, found themselves with their own charter airline. They weren't actually in charge. Still less did they busy themselves with the nuts and bolts: taking reservations, ensuring the flights were full, and processing the paperwork, with both Caledonian and the passengers. All that was run by Annette and Mike Barham's wife, Miff. She took the bookings, since the Barhams were one of the few families on the base with a home telephone. Annette, alongside a day job doing typing for the High Commissioner's office, handled most of the rest. And they soon established a schedule of once-a-month flights.

The first one, in July, did not seem to augur well. The plan was to stop for refuelling in Malta on the way to London. As

John stood alongside the aircraft, he was flanked by David Welsh, his second in command.

'What's the food like on board,' Welsh asked matter-of-factly.

'Food? What do you mean, food?' John replied.

'They need something, don't they? At least a cup of coffee.'

'No, they don't.'

'Of course they do, John,' Welsh replied. 'We better go and get some.'

And so they did, striding along the runway to the offices of Aden Airways in the civilian terminal.

'Where the hell is the food we ordered?' Welsh bluffed. And it worked. Within the hour, they were able to deliver a full complement of flight meals to the charter, which took off barely a half-hour later than scheduled.

Then, within an hour, it was back. One of the engines had caught fire. No harm, in the end, was done. But at the height of summer, it wasn't straightforward for Caledonian to locate and fly in a replacement aircraft, delaying the maiden flight of their new charter service by several days. And inevitably, by the time of the second flight in August, Group Captain Beetham took notice. Just as inevitably, Annette and Miff were summoned to his office, where one of his aides asked, in essence, how a couple of mere *women* could run a charter service. The women in question had little trouble allaying his doubts on that score. Still, it was clear that the very idea of RAF officers, or even their wives, running a private charter service did not sit well with the commander, and they decided that the September flight would be the last.

That was a source of disappointment to John, but nothing too acute. For to the extent his shifts left him with time or energy for freelance business endeavours, charter aircraft were not at the top of his to-do list. As so often before – and as would so often prove the case in the years ahead – the main attraction lay elsewhere.

His real interest was cars.

In another sign of what was to come, Annette was a full partner in what the two of them would look back on, years later, as their Aden Project.

The third partner in their endeavour was David Hyland, the junior officer in John's air-movements team, with whom John and Annette had become friends. In fact, a few months into their time at Khormaksar, Annette joined him for nearly a week in the French-ruled enclave of Djibouti, in East Africa, across the water from Aden. It was at the instigation of the wife of another officer in John's unit, who was working for the cigarette company British American Tobacco, and the occasion was a gymkhana event for which BAT was a sponsor. David Hyland, an accomplished horseback rider, was a member of the RAF's equestrian team and was going to compete in it. Ostensibly, Annette would be going along to work: handing out complimentary packets of Benson & Hedges. Still, it struck her as good fun, and John, who was on shift duty, could hardly object. The work part – which Annette carried out, at the sponsor's request, in a long, clingy white dress – was not a success. The French spectators seemed perfectly happy with their unfiltered *Gauloises*, and no amount of her charm seemed able to alter that. But attending the event, and savouring the fine food and drink offered alongside, was undeniably invigorating. It was a feeling Annette could hardly disguise on her return to Aden. Nor was it lost on John, who was waiting for her at the apartment when she got back. 'Boy, was he grumpy,' she recalled. 'That was *one* occasion on which John did not show that famous smile!'

Still, while John was not especially interested in David's horses, he *was* intrigued by something else that distinguished him from a lot of the other officers in Khormaksar. Given the insurgency, and the other limits on where and when you could drive, not many officers had their own motor cars. Yet some did. John and Annette had the use of a mundane Ford Zephyr Zodiac. Yet Hyland had bought a decidedly livelier vehicle from an officer heading back to England. It was an Austin-Healey Sprite convertible, with its pepped-up 950cc engine and distinctive 'frogeye' headlights.

It was British Racing Green. It looked immaculate. It did *not* drive immaculately, however. Both the engine and gearbox had seen better days. David had begun trying to fix it up himself, and had written away for the official handbook which all manufacturers provided for garages. But it was so densely laden with technical jargon that it might as well have been written in Japanese or Urdu. Besides, it assumed you'd have access to the kind of specialist tools available to a professional mechanic back home. It was John who saw the opportunity, and came up with the proposal. He suggested to David that he'd help strip down, repair and rebuild the Sprite ... and then publish a manual on exactly how it was done.

The idea had been percolating for months, and as John talked it through with Annette in ever greater detail, it became something quite different from the half-dozen-or-so other titles he had published since his first boarding-school booklet. Those were essentially illustrated references on building a kit-car, or souping up more modest production versions. This would be the full equivalent of the manufacturer's manual, but designed to be of use for ordinary car-owners. There was another important difference, which grew out of Annette's view, which John quickly came to accept, about why the Ford Anglia book that they'd completed before Aden hadn't made more than a publishing ripple. 'That wasn't a real *manual*,' she told him. 'It was an ordinary book.' She said for a manual, the pages had to be bigger. It needed photos, and illustrations as well, and they had to be positioned alongside the plain-English explanation of the work needed to attend to each part of the car.

John and Annette's four-storey block of flats, like the others along Ma'alla, had an open area in front that allowed a place to park. When David drove up with his Sprite, he and John lugged the engine and gearbox assembly up four flights of the narrow concrete stairway and into the Haynes's apartment. They lowered it onto the big trestle table in the spare bedroom. Over the next eight weeks – armed with the official Sprite manual, and the experience John had built up from his earlier car guides – they spent all their off-duty hours disassembling and repairing or refurbishing each part of the inner workings. John annotated each step and, with an Asahi Pentax camera he had purchased duty-free, photographed the entire process. When the work was done, they carried the assembly back downstairs and put it back in the Sprite. The last step was the taste test: David took it for a spin. He came back with an enthusiastic thumbs-up. Not only did it look like a sports car. Now it drove like one.

It took another six weeks for John to finish writing his 'owner's workshop' manuscript. At the start of the project, he'd had a stroke of particular good fortune. He had written to the British Motoring Corporation – the giant formed from the 1950s merger between William Morris and his rival Austin Motors. They made not only the Austin-Healey but the MG Midget, the line of Austin cars and the Morris Minor as well. Telling them, with the feigned innocence of a mere amateur, that he was writing a book about the Sprite, he asked whether it would be all right to include illustrations from the manufacturer's manual which David Hyland had been sent. BMC said yes. That meant he had access to professionally drawn diagrams. Annette now set about preparing each page of manuscript, aligning the margins, typing each page over again and putting the draft in final form, along with the pictures and illustrations. Then they sent it off to David Haynes in Yeovil, where a kind of Haynes family conveyor-belt swung into action. David printed several thousand copies on A4-sized sheets. He took them to his parents' house in batches. There, Harold and Vi collated them and walked them over, in a wicker shopping basket, to a more established Yeovil printer, Edward Snell & Sons, which bound them and added a thick paper cover.

The result was the first true Hayes Motor Manual.

Unlike the Ford Anglia book, it sold briskly. And to judge by everything John did during his final year in Aden, he fully intended that it would be the first of many. He soon churned out similar books on the MG Midget, the Austin A30 and the Morris Minor – all of which shared BMC's 'A-series' mechanics with the Sprite. A few months later, he was heartened to hear from his brother that he'd found at least slightly more salubrious quarters for his printing business: co-leasing a one-time Yeovil jewellery factory, less than a mile away, with an auto-accessory dealer. But John was thinking bigger. Through a friend back in England, he heard that a Co-op grocery store in the village of Lower Odcombe, west of Yeovil, had gone out of business and hoped to sell its premises, an old building that had originally consisted of three separate cottages. He bought it, sight unseen. He and David then came to an arrangement under which, in return for a monthly rent that was pretty much what he'd been paying in the old jewellery shop, the ground floor would accommodate the printing works and the latest iteration of the Sporting Motorists Bookshop, freeing Harold and Vi, and their garage, from that burden. The upper floor in Odcombe would be set aside for living quarters for David, as well as storage space, and for an office, from which John hoped to run his publishing business full-time when, at some future point, his service in the RAF came to an end.

Yet when – and even *if* – that would happen was anything but clear when he and Annette returned to Britain in November 1966. The only thing they could know for sure was that their lives were about to change dramatically.

Far from leaving the service, John was about to take his next step up the RAF ladder. And both he and his wife were also about to take on a new personal responsibility. For Annette was nearly six months pregnant.

*Chapter Seven*

# THE BIG DECISION

Their new home *was* a beauty spot. The spa town of Harrogate, nestled among the downs of North Yorkshire, had first become a magnet for visitors in the 1500s, when word spread about the curative properties of its waters. Yet over the centuries, something else, too, had drawn people from all across England and beyond. There was a special feel, a quality, about the place. It was quiet. It was sedate. It was genteel. It was the perfect antidote to the drain and din of city life. It offered a kind of escape – most famously of all, perhaps, for Agatha Christie, who, upon discovering that her husband was having an affair, provoked eleven days of national hysteria in the 1920s by simply disappearing without a trace. She finally turned up in Harrogate's venerable Old Swan hotel, back then called the Swan Hydropathic. The world's most famous mystery writer had checked in as a 'Mrs Teresa Neele', from Cape Town.

Harrogate was, undeniably, a very pleasant place to be pregnant. But for both John and Annette, it was also startlingly, unsettlingly different from the life they'd recently left behind. Aden, despite the pressures and occasional hardships, had been a place of adventure, energy, excitement. And, most of the time, enjoyment as well. Still just twenty-eight years old, they were bound to find Harrogate a bit *too* sedate.

For John, his new assignment only made the transition more difficult. As postings back in England went, it was, for most returning officers, an eminently desirable one, not least because of the attractions of Harrogate as a place to live. John's frustration was partly because he was moving from an operational role, on the largest British air base in the world, into a mere desk job. Yet it was also the *kind* of desk job. He remained an officer in the air force. But the group of weathered buildings where he would now be reporting to work each morning – on St George's Street, in the middle of town, not too far from the Old Swan – came under the purview of the Ministry of Defence. And the work it did was anything but operational. It was in charge of supply and procurement for the air force: essentially a higher-rank version of the first job he'd had in the RAF, in Bruggen.

The last time that MoD Harrogate had played an operational role was during the Second World War. Then, it had been home to both the training programme for the Women's Auxiliary Air Force and a so-called 'reception centre' for young RAF pilots who had gone on courses overseas before joining the war on the continent. In fact – and John might at least have enjoyed the irony, had he known – one of them was a twenty-one-year-old pilot, newly promoted to flying officer, who was soon sent on from Harrogate to fly Lancaster bomber missions over Berlin. His name was Michael Beetham.

Since it was an MoD facility, John and his colleagues also didn't wear air force uniforms. They were expected to dress more like middle-level City bankers. So he strode in each day in a suit and a bowler hat, with an umbrella, ever-ready for the not-infrequent Harrogate rain, clutched under his arm. He felt – and, as Annette was not beyond pointing out, also looked – faintly ridiculous.

He was not blind to the practical advantages of his position. He was an air force officer in good standing, still on his way up the ranks. He had every prospect of earning an increasingly comfortable living and retiring on a generous pension. Those considerations mattered, especially at a time when he and Annette were expecting a child, and when his air force salary was also helping him build up his business on the side. Besides, at the start of his time in Harrogate, his main focus, beyond making sure he was doing his job competently, was on his increasingly pregnant wife. And in the early hours of the nineteenth of February, three months after their arrival, Annette gave birth to their son. The delivery, after a difficult labour, was at a maternity home not far from their house. John was at her side, and, as soon as the midwife allowed, he cradled the child in his arms. They named him John Harold Coleman Haynes, but nicknamed him John Junior. His Aunt Jillie commented that they couldn't call him that, so he became JJ, and as he got older, just plain J.

John did his best to stay engaged at work, but it wasn't easy. He was besotted with little JJ and, while Annette was much more involved with the day-to-day demands of caring and cooking and cleaning, he did his best to help out. He also tried not to bring too much of the frustration from the MoD job home each night. Yet it wouldn't exactly have taken Agatha Christie to work out that he found the work not just tedious, but often pointless. From the time JJ was a couple of months old, he and Annette began talking seriously about whether he should leave the service. He kept running through the pros and cons. Annette was keenly aware of both. She made it clear she'd have no qualms about the potential risks in his simply quitting and throwing all his, and their, energies into his still-precarious motor-manual company. After all, she had some experience of business uncertainties: she'd spent much of her early youth watching her mother move from managing one inn to another, and her teenage years in the hotel in Ireland. But ultimately, she said, it would have to be John's decision. 'And it seems to me,' she said, 'that it's time to make up your mind one way or the other.'

The turning point came at work a couple of days later. He found himself dealing with a request to seek suppliers for a large quantity of boots for the air force, only to discover that a colleague in the office next to his had been detailed to find buyers for *surplus* boots. Still, both he and Annette agreed that he shouldn't just up and leave immediately. They had an infant child.

They would have to get a clearer idea of how they'd finance the move, and their lives, once they left Harrogate. Not least, they would also need a place to live.

John began using weekends to take care of that part at least, as well as keeping his eye on the business. Shortly after arriving in Harrogate, they'd bought a cute, perky little Triumph TR4. Now, he began using it for weekend trips back to Somerset with Annette and JJ and their home-scouting excursions. Immediately after work on Friday, he'd start it up, make the nearly six-hour journey down through the whole of England, staying at his parents' house, and then patrolling the surrounding countryside for likely properties. They found a few that drew their interest, but none seemed quite right, until one spring afternoon they passed through a picture-book village a few miles north of Yeovil. It was a tiny place, with just a few hundred souls. It was called West Camel. This had nothing to do with the animal: there was not a dromedary in sight. More likely, it was because it straddled a tributary of the River Cam, although the original, Saxon name, *Cantmeel*, simply meant 'bare ridge'. And on one edge, there was a lovely old stone farmhouse – or, to be exact, *half* of the farmhouse – which was for sale. There was a barn on the property, perfect, John figured, for storing, or maybe at some point even printing, his books.

It was lucky he hadn't already left the air force. He and Annette were going to need a mortgage. Even though his Sprite manuals and the others that they'd finished in Aden were selling almost as quickly as the Odcombe press could print them, no bank was going to lend them money on the basis of John's back-of-the-envelope calculations of his company's future prospects. He managed instead to secure the loan by showing his RAF payslips. The purchase was completed by the start of summer 1967. With considerable work needed on their new home, which was called Camway House, they wouldn't be able to move in until the autumn. But there could no longer be any doubt that they were leaving Harrogate – which left only the small matter of John telling the air force.

At first, his commanding officer thought it must have been some sort of joke. Whatever John's feelings about the work he was doing in Harrogate, he was being paid well, something surely of particular importance to a new parent. He was certain to become, at the least, a squadron leader if he stayed in the air force. And when his career was over, he'd be able to draw on a good government pension. When John insisted that he'd already thought of all that, but still felt it was right to leave, his superiors were decidedly unamused. They couldn't keep him from leaving, after the proper notice period, in early August. But though officers with his level of seniority were quite often given a severance payment to help ease them into civilian life, it was made clear to departing Flight Lieutenant John Haynes that he'd have to leave cold turkey.

His superiors weren't the only ones who questioned the wisdom of John's decision to cast off the certainties of his RAF life for the potentially choppy waters of running his book business full time. As Annette recalls, all but a handful of their friends thought it was not just ill-advised, but downright 'crazy'. And at least one family member – John's mother, Vi – urged him to think again. Though years later, to John's amusement, she'd insist she *always* knew that leaving the air force was the right thing for him to do, her concerns were understandable. She'd had painful personal experience in her early life of the perils of lacking the kind of stability and structure which the air force afforded.

At least as John packed up for their final drive south – in a battered Bedford van he'd borrowed from the printing works in Lower Odcombe – they had the reassurance of having somewhere to live while they waited for Camway to be made habitable. In a mirror image of his brother's latest career choice, David Haynes had decided to *return* to the air force. He'd enjoyed making a success of his printing business, and helping John restart the momentum of his publishing business. But he didn't see printing as his life's work and he hoped – rightly, as things turned out – to use a further stint in the RAF to acquire the broader financial, managerial, legal and technical skills taught to its aspiring paymaster-generals. The timing made sense for both brothers: John bought the printing operation when David left in June, and the apprentice whom David had hired was able to carry on its operations. And as a bonus, the flat in Odcombe was now vacant, allowing John, Annette and JJ to move in.

It wasn't much of a home. Accommodation consisted of a single room, barely big enough for a bed and JJ's cot. The rest of the upper floor had become an unruly storage area, piled high with books and assorted printing supplies. There was no hot water and no inside loo either, just a chemical toilet at the bottom of the garden. Two or three times a week, he and Annette would drive into Yeovil and bathe JJ – and themselves – at Harold and Vi's house. But it was fine. 'It was fun, in fact,' Annette recalled. 'You have to remember, we were very young. There was this feeling of kind of camping out, and the fact that we were starting something new.'

Still, it did wear on them over time, something she fully realised only in October, when they finally moved into Camway. 'That was *lovely* … I'll always remember the joy on the first night we were there. It was an old-fashioned house, and the bathroom was old-fashioned as well. It had this huge tub. Very deep. I filled it to the top with hot water, and I sank into it. And I thought: this is wonderful. My own bath!'

Yet despite the genuine novelty of his first few step-by-step manuals – even despite the fact there were obviously car-owners ready to buy them – there was no guarantee John would be able to build a viable business around them. All he needed to do to be reminded of how far he still had to go was to walk into a high-street bookstore pretty much anywhere in England and pick up one of the many titles published by a company called Autobooks.

They weren't quite as detailed as Haynes's manuals. They lacked the step-by-step photos. They didn't involve the authors' physically stripping down the cars they wrote about, reassembling them piece by piece, and chronicling the process in a way that a non-specialist owner could easily follow. But they were a substantial improvement on the manufacturers' handbooks. They were well written. And they sold: widely, consistently, in large numbers. On repeated occasions, the first one a few months before he and Annette were married, John would insist on a detour when they were visiting her parents in Worthing, on the south coast. They would drive on to Brighton, a few miles further east, where Autobooks was headquartered. Then they would park outside the factory and watch as large post-office vans pulled up outside to take on board sackful after sackful of Autobooks guides for distribution around the country. 'Look at all those books!' John exclaimed, in a mix of astonishment and envy.

During their early months at Camway, he fizzed with energy, and with an obvious determination to build up his own business to a point where, some day, Autobooks might glance admiringly in *his* direction. It was slow going, but if he ultimately fell short, it wasn't going to be for lack of ambition. About six months after they'd moved into the half-farmhouse, the other part came on the market. John bought it, too. He applied for planning permission to use the barn for 'light industrial' purposes: specifically, to move the printing operation there, which would leave Lower Odcombe with the bookshop and expanded space for offices. And he and Annette began planning, one by one, more of the new-style owners' manuals: on Austins and Minis and Fords – even a revamp of the pre-Aden flop, the Ford Anglia book, to make it into the kind of owner-friendly manual they'd now definitively settled on.

At least for the time being, however, the publications were still produced in a decidedly old-style way. Annette did the typing, helped John with the accounts and rustled up hot lunches for the first handful of young apprentices they had begun to hire locally. Odcombe did the printing. Harold and Vi pitched in with collating the pages. The one early change was to enlist a wider, informal network to help with that task. It consisted mostly of women who were employed from their homes in Yeovil's then-thriving glove industry, and who were happy to earn a little extra money.

The feeling of moving ahead, of growing, the sense of building something special bit by bit, extended to their family life as well. For by the end of 1967, Annette was well into her second pregnancy, and in late April 1968, she delivered their second son, Marc – a transition which, typically, was accompanied by another addition to John's motoring possessions: a family-friendly Vauxhall Victor estate car.

'He looks *so* like John,' Vi gushed. Nor was she alone in remarking – from the time he first began to play, and talk, crawl and finally walk – on how he seemed to have inherited a healthy dose of his father's determination. And his bright light beam of a smile.

On one bright winter afternoon when he was about a year-and-a-half, Annette, who was helping oversee the latest refurbishment work on the barn-turned-printing-operation at Camway, suddenly realised that both Marc and JJ were gone. Rushing toward the metal gate that led to the lane out front, she was relieved to see her younger boy toddling away just outside. 'Where's JJ?' she asked, at which point Marc, turning toward her and beaming, proclaimed: 'JJ gone!' And he might well have been had it not been for a JCB at the top of the hill behind the house, evidently abandoned for the day by the crew of workers resurfacing the busy nearby road. JJ was happily clambering on top of it.

Yet shortly before Marc's second birthday, she and John became worried that something was not quite right about him physically. As Annette related to their GP, he seemed occasionally unsteady on his feet, even for a toddler. His neck seemed a bit stiff, too, and he had begun to hold his head angled slightly forward. In April of 1970, the GP referred them to Dr Nigel Royston, a consultant paediatrician at Yeovil General Hospital. A singularly forward-looking physician, Royston had just opened an 'opportunity' centre where both able and disabled children could learn and play together. It was the first such facility in Britain. Their initial meeting was, on balance, reassuring. From the outset, John and Annette liked Dr Royston, and, no less important, Marc obviously liked him too. He was kind, careful, and obviously knowledgeable. Marc did have a physical problem, the doctor said. And while it was impossible to say definitively at this stage, he thought it was probably a peripheral nerve condition – polyneuritis – and that Marc's symptoms would, over time, improve.

'Would it be safe for us to take him on a family holiday in a few weeks' time?' Annette asked. It would be their first real time away since leaving the RAF. Nearly all their time, energy, and resources had been directed to settling in Somerset and getting the business on its feet. The plan was to cross the Channel and head south across the continent to the Costa Brava in northern Spain, where they'd honeymooned seven years before. John was especially looking forward to the drive. The TR4 was obviously not suited to the task. Besides, it had been effectively repurposed over the past year, and was being used to deliver his car-manuals to specialist motor retailers around the south and west of England. The thought of using the Vauxhall estate didn't exactly make his heart sing either. But he had recently purchased a ten-year-old Jaguar XK150 DHC – a car that would remain dear to him for the remainder of his life – and he was eager to put it through its paces.

'A holiday should be no problem,' Dr Royston replied, smiling. Just bundle up Marc, he said. Watch for any worsening of his condition, of course, but he should be fine. 'Come see me when you get back.'

The Jaguar had a long sleek front, with the iconic cat leaping from its bonnet, and a 3.4-litre engine which, if it weren't for the two infants on board, John would surely have been tempted to bring to its maximum 130mph at some stage along the way. Instead, they took special care, cosseting Marc's kiddie seat in the front, next to John, amid a small mountain of bags. Technically, the car was a four-seater, but there were only two narrow perches in the back, into which Annette squeezed herself with JJ, who had just recently turned three. Since they kept the convertible top closed for the journey, at least wind and cold weren't problems.

The only hitch came as they were crossing the Pyrenees, and they suddenly got caught in a torrential downpour. While the body of the Jaguar still looked in near-mint condition, the innards were evidently feeling their age. The front of the car stayed dry enough. But it turned out that the metal underpinning of the back seats was virtually gone. As Annette hugged JJ close to her, water began seeping, then spewing up from below. By the time the rain eased and they pulled to the side of the road, both of them were soaked through.

The Costa Brava, once they got there, was as lovely as they remembered it. Marc, smiling and laughing, showed every sign of enjoying the whole adventure. But while John and Annette obviously were encouraged by his high spirits, and hopeful that their obviously unwell two-year-old would indeed get better over time, Annette was becoming more unsettled. It wasn't that Marc's condition had changed in any dramatic way. The symptoms were still the same: the stiffly held neck, bent forward toward his chest. But she couldn't help noticing that it was bent a little bit *more* further forward. And more worrying, Marc seemed increasingly disinclined, or maybe just unable, to raise his head upright.

So it was with this nagging concern that, the day after they returned home from Spain, she took him back to see Dr Royston.

Still, nothing had prepared her for what came next.

*Chapter Eight*

# GROWING PAINS

D r Royston's familiar, reassuring smile welcomed Annette and Marc into his consulting room. He lifted the child from her arms and held him to his chest. For a few moments, he said nothing. He stroked Marc's head. Then, quietly, he said: 'Mrs Haynes, has he raised his head at all lately?' Annette paused, and replied: 'No. Not in the past few weeks.' Nodding, the doctor placed his hand on Marc's forehead. Then, he gradually manoeuvred Marc's head backwards. In a moment of horror that Annette would never forget, she said she could actually *hear* the bones crunching back into alignment, and she watched as her child, without so much as a sound, went utterly limp in the doctor's arms. 'What have you *done* to my baby?' she remembered crying out. 'I just couldn't help it. It was horrible.'

'He's going to be all right,' Dr Royston assured her, 'but we're going to have to take him to Frenchay' – the large NHS hospital in Bristol, some 50 miles north of Yeovil. 'They have emergency facilities there. They'll see him, and observe him. We'll need tests.'

Since this was years before the age of the iPhone, it was nearly four hours later when she could finally get to a phone and call John to let him know what had happened: how Marc had been rushed by ambulance to Bristol, with Annette following in its slipstream, pushing the lumbering Vauxhall estate for all it was worth. How he'd been admitted through A & E and taken to a side ward, conscious but still inert and utterly quiet. And how the doctors still couldn't tell her precisely what was going on. 'They need to do tests, all sorts of tests,' she told John.

They did the tests, dozens of them, although the one exam that would have immediately been used today – an MRI – was still nearly as distant an innovation as the iPhone. At least, the family already had live-in help at home. Even before Marc's medical crisis, John and Annette had hired a young woman named Sally White in order to ensure they could care for their two small children while also moving to expand their still fairly makeshift business into a real, viable company. But JJ himself was still a toddler, and now, of all times, their priorities were to make sure they were present for both the children. During the two weeks or so of tests, Annette drove up to Bristol each day and sat by Marc's bedside. He was alert, but still just lay there quietly. The most wrenching part of it for her was that, while the nurses could manage to get a few words out of him, and even a smile, he had only a steely silence for his mother. He wouldn't even look at her. 'The message was obvious: *I* was the one who'd landed him there,' Annette would recall. 'I understood. But it was painful.'

The *real* pain, however, came once the tests were done. And as she and John listened to the doctors' diagnosis, the hope that had been sustaining them for months – the belief that their child's 'peripheral nerve' problems would gradually ease – was replaced by dread. Marc had a series of cysts that were compressing his spinal cord. It was a condition called syringomyelia, risking not only a loss of feeling in his hands, and a progressively worsening contraction of his back and neck, but paralysis. The surgeons at Frenchay proposed to perform a pair of operations, two weeks apart: laminectomies, to pare away part of the infant's vertebral bone in his spinal canal. The aim was to try to free up space, allow the spinal cord to decompress and free his neck. 'Could he die?' Annette asked, only to get a professionally hedged reply that left both parents preparing themselves for the worst.

The days leading up to the first operation, and the fortnight before the second, were excruciating. 'We really thought we were going to lose our wonderful little boy,' Annette recalled. The fact that they didn't was, of course, a huge relief. They took heart, too, from the fact that after the procedures he seemed able to move his neck more freely. Yet as Annette continued her daily commutes to Bristol during his recovery, it was already clear he might have to live with severe disabilities. He could not sit unaided. He couldn't walk. He couldn't move his arms or legs, only his right hand. The longer-term prognosis was also deeply uncertain. But as John and Annette prepared to take him home from the hospital, the lead surgeon told them: 'I'll say one thing about your baby boy. He is *very* stubborn ... And that will either work well for him, or the other way. I hope it will work well.'

There was a surreal feeling to the months that followed. As soon as they'd brought him back home, they had a special high-seat made to support his back. Although in the absence of anything resembling reliable evidence, they kept telling themselves – and doing all they could to convey to three-year-old JJ – that Marc had been ill, but that he was now beginning a road to recovery.

Amid all of that, they pushed ahead with as much, if not more, determination as before with the transformation of their business. Even an armchair psychologist would suspect at least some measure of denial was at work: an attempt to quiet the pain, and the fear, they felt about Marc's condition by immersing themselves in these day-to-day demands. But in a purely practical sense, they had little other option. John was in no position to re-enlist for a *third* time in the RAF, even if he had wanted to, which he most definitely didn't. And the moves to expand the publishing operation were by now well under way. They had ramped up the production of the car manuals and, only a few months before Marc's emergency, had hired an eighteen-year-old named Rod Grainger as an 'editorial assistant'. A self-proclaimed petrolhead, he'd been working at the Yeovil-based Westland Aircraft company. Now, with planning permission in hand, they were well on their way to moving the printing works from Odcombe into the barn at Camway, and had lined up four other apprentices to handle expanded production there.

Also a young woman from West Camel named Sandra MacKinnon. At first, she'd been taken on to help Annette keep the accounts and the paperwork in order, and she soon became John's secretary and all-round personal assistant – an increasingly indispensable role she'd continue to play for the rest of his working life. 'His second wife,' Annette often quipped.

They were also turning out new Haynes manuals for Camway to print. That was the most important, and most labour-intensive, part. There was no getting around the process. They would choose a model to write about, often borrowed from a friend or a dealer. Then they'd take it apart, either at Camway or a friend's garage, and put it back together piece by piece, documenting and photographing every step along the way. John himself remained the key to that part. This was not because he was a professional mechanic; it was because he *wasn't*. He did have basic engineering skills. He knew, and loved, cars. But he had no more formal training in finding, replacing or repairing their insides than most of the car-owners who were buying the manuals. He was, in a real sense, like them. That was what made Haynes Manuals different. That was what, in those first few years after leaving the RAF, allowed him to sell the new manuals almost as quickly as he could print them.

And his determination – bordering, sometimes, on obsession – to ramp up the business could hardly have come at a more fortuitous time. Britain was finally beginning to fully recover from the economic burdens of the Second World War. Private car sales were one dramatic barometer of the country's recovery. In 1970, for the first time, more than half of British households owned an automobile. In the two decades that followed, that figure would rise to two-thirds of the population. It was a trend that transformed the way people lived. It gave them a new sense of freedom. Confidence. Self-worth. And it also soon gave many first-time buyers something of a problem: what to do when their prized possessions, saved up for and striven for, went wrong. The answer, for an inexorably expanding number, became a Haynes Manual.

At the beginning of the 1970s, nearly all of Haynes's sales were still by mail order, in response to ads in car magazines or, more each month, from word-of-mouth. But every few weeks, he and Annette had begun making the four-hour drive east to London and, on the southern edge of the capital, dropping off an increasingly large consignment at a specialist motoring bookshop called Chater & Scott. They had also taken on two new employees. One was a full-time accountant called Frank Day. He was an obvious necessity, given the speed at which the business was growing. But John would never entirely break a habit developed in the early days of the business, at the time when Harold was handling the mail order from the 'bookshop' in his Yeovil garage. Back then, he'd kept a handwritten ledger of every manual sold, every expense incurred, every penny banked. Accountant or not, that urge would never entirely leave him.

The other hire was their first salesman, a young man named John Hall. Every week, he and Annette would cram the Vauxhall estate with manuals and, as Hall set out on a zigzag itinerary that took in auto parts stores and garages all over the south of England, John would give him his marching orders: 'Come back when you've sold them all.'

In August 1971, John finally felt the need to come up for breath; for all of the family to get away again after the most fraught year, personally and professionally, of their shared lives.

The US airline Pan Am had launched a house-swap programme as a new way of promoting their transatlantic flights, and John sorted out an exchange with an American family. The Americans got Camway, which they found wonderfully, quaintly English – especially since the swap included Annette's latest everyday car, a Ford Capri, which they good-naturedly described afterwards as a 'motorised roller skate'. The Haynes family got a delightful family home in the village of Port Jefferson, on the northern shore of Long Island some sixty miles east of New York City, complete with an equally compact, though decidedly more powerful, AMC Gremlin. 'All bonnet and no car,' Annette quipped.

Their Long Island escape was not entirely without its glitches. In what, for John, was a truly extraordinary turn of events, he discovered once they'd landed in New York that he had somehow forgotten to bring along the key for the Gremlin. A car key, for him, was an item of near-iconic importance. He would always carry the full complement for all of his vehicles on a single chain, from which he could not bear to be parted. In sorting out the problem, moreover, he would end up having to violate the two iron rules which friends back home had told him he must hold to on the trip: first, never trust a New York taxi driver; second, *certainly* never approach a New York cop.

At the urging of Annette – who was sitting outside the terminal with their luggage and two increasingly tired young children – he did finally succumb to the offer of a nearby cab driver to drive them out to the Long Island home. He was enormously helpful, even stopping at a grocery store to make sure they would have basic provisions, and checking that the borrowed house's utilities were all in working order.

The next morning, John got a duplicate key from an AMC garage and took a train back to the airport to collect the car. At first, all went smoothly. But after he'd backed it out of its space in the parking lot, he couldn't manage to get it into forward gear. He got out, cast his eyes about, and realised that the only person close enough to ask for help was a policeman. With great reluctance, John approached him. 'Excuse me, sir,' he said, in a consciously reinforced English accent, 'but I appear to have a problem. I can't get this car out of reverse gear.' The policeman smiled. 'You're in luck, my friend,' he said. 'My son's got a Gremlin.' And he proceeded to open the bonnet and point out a small metal lever, which, he said, sometimes got stuck.

Still, the trip was bookended by two undeniable highs. At the outset, back in England, they'd arrived late for their flight from Heathrow and, to the children's delight, they were all upgraded to first class.

On the day before their return home, something even more welcome occurred. For the first time since Marc had left hospital, almost exactly a year earlier, there was the first sign that he might actually be able to walk again. Back at Camway, Annette would occasionally help him to his feet and then position his little hands on the back of a wooden chair, in the hope that he would get used to the idea of standing on his own and eventually walking. That hadn't happened. But now, on the wooden floor of the Port Jefferson cottage, the chair suddenly slipped forward an inch or two. At first with a look of alarm, but then with a broad smile, Marc took a few steps forward. And then a few more.

As if that were not encouragement enough, they encountered another bit of serendipity on the drive back from Heathrow to Camway a couple of days later. As they were passing through the Somerset village of Sparkford, just a couple of miles from home, John noticed a 'For Sale' sign on an old, disused creamery complex. For months, he'd been taking out leases on an assortment of properties around the Yeovil area to use as warehouse space for the growing number of manuals they were printing. Now – assuming, of course, that the price for such a large property wasn't beyond them – he had happened upon a site where they could store them all. Print them, too. There might even be space to take apart the cars, photograph them, and put them back together.

And on all of those things, he would turn out to be right. Yet what he couldn't, or at least didn't, anticipate was the challenge of holding their own lives together along the way.

*Chapter Nine*

# ON THE MARKET

John Haynes worked hard and played hard. That had been true ever since he'd left boarding school for the RAF. But never before or after would he display the sheer intensity that marked both parts of his life in the years after he spotted the 'For Sale' poster on the abandoned creamery. For Britain, the 1970s were a time of economic and political tumult. For Haynes, too, they held their share of tremors. But they would also turn out to be his defining decade. The personal wealth, and recognition, came only later. But without the near-manic drive that now consumed him – and without navigating, and surviving, the pressures it brought upon him and those closest to him – they might not have come at all.

It was as if he was entering one of his old weekend auto races, in the lead, but only just, and knowing that everything now depended on pushing ahead with every fibre of his being. Just as on the track, the race itself set his pulse and adrenalin throbbing. That, too, had been true from the very first steps he'd taken to build his business in his RAF days. But this was different. He now was absolutely certain of what he wanted his company to be, and how he saw it developing. The core would be his Haynes Motor Manuals – not just any fix-it guides, but uniquely prepared for, explained for, and illustrated for both motor enthusiasts and ordinary car-owners. Even at this early stage, nothing gave him greater pleasure than stories of how his books *connected*, on a personal level, with the readers he was creating them for. In later years, he'd draw even deeper enjoyment in hearing from, meeting, and talking to those for whom owning a car had become inseparable from their well-thumbed, oil-stained Haynes manuals in the boot.

But all that was still part of a vision. This final lap of the track, in John's mind, was about making it a reality. And he was thinking big. First, he needed to sustain the momentum he'd begun building around the manuals. By now, he had around twenty-five of them on his list. But he still saw himself not just as a manuals man. He would be a *publisher*, hoping to add other motoring titles, real *books* about cars and those who drove them. And he wanted his company not just to outpace Autobooks or other competitors and become the go-to source for British car-owners. He knew that for Haynes Publishing to develop into a major player – let alone become the publishing equivalent of boyhood hero William Morris's car empire – he would need an entrée into the single largest car-owning community in the world: North America. All that was part of what now had him straining and sprinting toward the chequered flag.

It was not about the money, or at least not about personal profit. Since setting up in Somerset, the business had begun bringing in sums he could barely have imagined a few years earlier. He was printing several thousand manuals each week, and selling pretty much all of them. But he kept only a small part of the revenues: to support the family, allow for excursions to nearby restaurants or, more often, pubs. The only personal luxury he allowed himself was his cars, especially the Jaguar XK that he'd bought a couple of years earlier and a more recent acquisition: a sleek white Jaguar E-Type, which he soon had repainted in an eye-catching yellow. By far most of the earnings were being ploughed back into the business: redoing the barn at Camway, leasing space for warehousing, hiring young apprentices, buying new equipment. And now, if all went well, buying the property in Sparkford.

The Creamery, as the locals called it, was well past its post-First World War prime. It was a jumble of gable-roofed buildings that meandered back from a front gate, all of them sorely in need of fresh plaster and paint. They also smelled – in fact, *reeked* – of stale milk. Little wonder, then, that the owners, Unigate – having merged a few years earlier with another of the country's main dairy companies – were now interested in getting the property off the books. John did the deal within weeks, at a fraction of the cost he'd have had to pay for space in one of the business parks dotted around the Yeovil area.

In the months that followed, he shifted into overdrive. He set about airing out, and in some parts hollowing out, Sparkford; rebuilding, replastering, repainting; then moving the printing operation from the barn at Camway. About a year later, the new Sparkford base was formally inaugurated, though getting the printing fully transferred, with updated equipment, and outfitting the space for disassembling and reassembling the cars, would be completed gradually over a period of another six months or so. By then, he was able to churn out around 8,000 manuals every week. The publication list was also growing. Within months of the move to Sparkford, the fiftieth manual would appear. He also managed to secure a distribution agreement with major cash-and-carry outlets and, since some of the largest ones were in the north of England, he bought an old tobacco warehouse in Leeds to handle the storage and distribution in the north. And he took his first step towards making a mark not just in manuals but more mainstream motor publishing: purchasing the century-old publishing firm G.T. Foulis. Though not specialising in motoring – veering off into everything from aviation fuel to one book on 'the stresses and strains of soil' – Foulis did publish a number of motoring titles that enjoyed near-iconic status among enthusiasts. Even more importantly, for John, owning Foulis would give him a path into mainstream booksellers.

But he worked hard and played hard. Either of them, at the pace and intensity with which John was living his life, would have been taxing. The combination, even for a man who was still in his early thirties, was bound to take its toll. The playing part had begun almost from the moment they'd moved into Camway, when he and Annette were still in their late twenties. They soon built up a group of a couple of dozen partying friends. They were all around their own age, and mostly single. Though John was no longer racing cars, he did still follow the racing scene, and some of their regular companions were weekend racers. Others, they met on their regular Saturday-night outings at an assortment of local pubs. Their favourite was a place called the Cross Keys, a few miles down the road from Camway in Sherborne, whose owners soon became valued, and indulgent, friends. Once the pub closed for the night, they'd often move on to a place called the 393 Club, located, bizarrely, in the little village of Ilchester, seven miles or so in the other direction from West Camel. It stayed open till nearly dawn, and offered not only drinking but dancing. On some weekends, they'd simply party at Camway. John and Annette would often wake up on Sunday morning to find at least two or three of their guests sprawled out on chairs, sofas, or a convenient patch of carpet downstairs.

But by the time John bought the creamery, he had not just one small child but two, with the younger one, Marc, battling his way back from a pair of emergency operations and just starting, unsteadily, to walk again. And then, a few weeks later, Annette discovered she was pregnant with a third. Nor did things get easier. A few months later, Marc endured two spells of tonsillitis. The antibiotics worked, but in each case, he suddenly lost the use of his legs again for several days. Annette and John, understandably upset, tried to get the doctors to remove the child's tonsils. But at the time, that was considered excessive, and there was an additional concern about the effects of such an operation, and the anaesthetic it required.

An older, more settled John Haynes would almost certainly have slowed down the frantic pace of his life, or at least tried. Even before Annette's pregnancy, and Marc's latest health scare, he'd always unfailingly carved out time at the end of each working day to spend with his children. But he could no more dial back the headlong efforts to expand his business than pull his car into the pits a few hundred metres from the finish line. Nor did he – *could* he, perhaps – entirely dispense with playing hard as well.

The crisis point, when it came, was almost accidental. John, through a combination of lack of exercise and generous helpings of lager and scotch, had been putting on weight for several years. He was not fat, but he was conscious of having lost the trim, dapperly uniformed look of his air force days. His brother David, of course, was back in the RAF, and *his* weight was going in the other direction. On one visit home, he told John how he'd been prescribed diet pills by the base physician, and had lost eight or nine kilos. John, of course, promptly got their family doctor to follow suit. The result was by far the most difficult period in his and Annette's marriage. The diet prescription was essentially amphetamines: speed. The side-effects of the pills, alone, might have been serious. But with a couple of beers thrown in, or a glass of his favourite whisky, they were no doubt worse. Within days, he began behaving erratically. He would suddenly get in his E-Type and disappear for hours on end, then return very late at night boasting to Annette how he'd pushed it to its limits, screaming through tight bends, and breaking the speed limit at will. This went on for several weeks. It stopped only when Annette noticed a newspaper article about similar cases among air force officers who'd been prescribed the diet medication. She promptly called the doctor, and said, as she would recall to a friend years later: 'Don't you *dare* give him any more!'

Yet even without the diet pills, juggling his non-stop working life with a young, growing family would remain a challenge. His family did unquestionably matter to him. Home mattered. Over the course of his life, the only serious competitor for his affections was – at times – his business. The pubbing and clubbing *seemed* important, and there was no doubt that, in the moment, he truly delighted in it. But those who were closest to him – Annette, David, his small circle of truly intimate friends – all say that John's revelry masked something more complex in him. Yes, he partied. Not only that, he was almost invariably the life of the party: full of smiles and, the word you most often hear from those who spun in social orbit around him, *bonhomie*.

He had a gift for humour as well, and an engaging ability to make it about laughing *with* people rather than at them. The totemic example was, in their mid-1970s excursions to the 393 Club, when the sound system would begin blaring out the Carly Simon hit 'You're so Vain'. In shared refrain, the others soon took to shouting: 'Johnny, they're playing your song!'

'But the bonhomie actually hid a reserve,' Annette would recall years later. John Haynes was an innately private man, much more comfortable in a small group of friends and family than on a public stage. The whirling, socialising side of him, much as he enjoyed it, required an act of will. It also goes a long way to explaining his fondness – his need – for a couple of jars of lager, or glasses of whisky, to ease him into party mode. It was a habit that, particularly when the pressures of his life intensified, sometimes threatened to spill into excess, until, years later, he gave up alcohol for good.

And now, the pressures were mounting. At home, there was a period of unalloyed joy, with the birth of their third child, Christopher. Marc also appeared to be making progress, step by halting step. Yet a couple of months later, around the time of his fifth birthday, he was hit by another bout of tonsillitis. Just as before, the antibiotics took care of the infection. Again, he lost the use of his legs. But this time, it became clear as the days and weeks passed, the loss would be permanent. The tiny walking sticks were packed away, and he was fitted with a wheelchair.

For John, the setback was especially difficult because – except, very occasionally with Annette – he kept all the worry inside him. David made one of his family visits back from his air force base shortly afterwards. John did, briefly, confide that it now seemed as if Marc would be fortunate to live into his teens. But when David tried, gently, to inquire further – about the cause of the disability, the operations, the prospect for future treatment – John simply changed the subject. And while there was no sign of any improvement, over the next couple of years there *was* some genuine reason for encouragement. It was what Marc's surgeon, after the second of his spine operations, had called his 'stubbornness'. It was a quality which, the doctor said, would 'either work well for him, or the other way'. It worked well. Despite his physical limitations, despite the frequent pain, Marc seemed absolutely determined to live as fully as any other child his age. He was almost always smiling. He was full of energy. Enrolled in the local infants' school – since he was adamantly opposed to going to Dr Royston's ground-breaking mixed-ability school – he happily adapted to a starring role at playtime. He and his wheelchair would alternately function as an imagined police car, a racing car or even, on one occasion, a tank. At home, he was no less assertive. Preparing dinner for the children one afternoon, Annette heard a shriek from the front room at Camway. When she rushed in, rather than finding that Marc had fallen over, as he would frequently do, he was deploying the wheelchair to pin a hapless J against the wall. It turned out that J had 'borrowed' one of his younger brother's toys. Marc's remarkable strength of will – his refusal to let his disability define his life – did not make the physical limitations any less real. But it did change things for the rest of the family: parents and siblings both. They were always alert to the possibility he would need their help. But as time passed, and Marc seemed only to grow in his determination to cope with most challenges on his own, the importance of his disability loomed less large for them as well.

Indeed, for a few years after Christopher was born, as if in some collective act of exhaling, John and Annette resumed their social life with a verve and vigour that recalled not just their first years in Somerset, but their motor-racing courtship of the early 1960s. John didn't go back on the weekend racing circuit. But he *did* go back to racing: not the round-the-track kind, but competitive hill-climbing and speed trials.

Just as in his first racing incarnation, he and Annette found themselves immersed in a new set of friends, who shared John's love for cars, for racing them, and for the fun, frivolity and general mischief that swirled around them. His two main racing buddies were a man named Andrew Jeans – known simply as AJ, and something of a local motoring celebrity – and John Blundell, another local racing enthusiast who would go on to carve out a distinguished career as a podiatrist in Australia. John and Blundell's first racer, for entering in the hill-climb competitions, was a Ford Escort RS1600, a lot like the one that would feature in the *Fast and Furious* films years later. But their speedster of choice was a gorgeous TVR Tuscan, which John bought and – along with Blundell and AJ – stripped down, fixed up and refitted with a 360bhp Holman and Moody V8 engine. By the time they'd finished, it was a fearsome beast, winning the speed trials competition at the former RAF base in Yeovilton and the annual seaside speed trials in Weston-super-Mare.

Their partying was nearly as high-octane as the racing, and it, too, often ended up involving cars. AJ remembers one night, when the whole gang was heading out to the 393 Club, when John took off ahead of them in a recently acquired Porsche 911.

Within seconds, they'd lost sight of him. By the time they caught up, several minutes later on a narrow lane they always took as a shortcut, John was grinning sheepishly, and helplessly, from the driver's seat. He'd taken a bend too quickly and gone up on a steep side bank. The Porsche was stranded on top of it, balanced like a very sleek and expensive seesaw.

Annette, in this instance, was making her separate way to the club, but she was usually a more-than-willing co-conspirator … up to a point. Another of their friends remembers one evening when they were out dancing, when the clock ticked past 2:30am. 'John,' she declared calmly, 'if you're not in that car park in five minutes, I'm leaving you here.'

He was.

Yet by the mid-1970s, John's campaign to make his long-term plan for Haynes Publishing a reality again began to overshadow all else. With more and more manuals being printed in greater and greater quantities, even Sparkford was straining at the seams. As John looked for ways to expand it, something he'd manage to do by buying an adjacent farm a year later, he leased additional office space in Ilchester, not too far from the 393 Club. In addition to the manuals, he was also reissuing some of G.T. Foulis's greatest motoring hits: on the history of the Ferrari, the Bugatti and the venerable Yorkshire-based Scott Motorcycle Company. But two much more fundamental aims were also now in his sights.

The first – with the help of Frank Day, the company accountant he'd hired at the start of the decade and had now made his managing director – was to begin plans to list Haynes Publishing on the London Stock Exchange. They retained the London banking firm Singer & Friedlander as advisers. John was determined that he and Annette would retain virtually full ownership of the company. But *if* he could keep building on the expansion of the past few years and draw the required interest in a share offering, the major injection of capital promised to transform the business, and their own lives.

Left to his own devices, he might well have made the move already. In every venture he'd attempted, beginning way back with the 'mushroom company' he'd set up during his holidays at Sutton Valence, John's approach to business decisions was a bit like a dog's to a bone. See it, size it up, grab it. But even without Day's cautionary advice, and Singer & Friedlander's, he could not fail to notice that Britain was living through a period of economic turbulence: widespread strikes, inflation and, most of all, the stark effects of the Arab oil embargo imposed during the 1973 Middle East war.

So now was *not* the time. For John, however, that merely increased the urgency of his second key expansion target: the United States. As with the flotation, he'd been thinking, talking, making piecemeal moves, for a couple of years. Twice, he'd signed an agreement with publishing companies in the States to distribute his manuals there. Twice, an initial spurt had fairly quickly fizzled. The logic of heading west with Haynes manuals struck him as inescapable. The US population at mid-decade was around 215 million, nearly four times Britain's. Many more Americans owned an automobile, or often two. Plus, large numbers of British cars had been exported to America. With minor tweaks – mostly, putting the steering wheel on the opposite side – a lot of his existing manuals could easily be adapted. And Haynes had also begun doing manuals for a number of Japanese imports, which were also being shipped in large numbers to America.

John was increasingly wedded to an idea of how they could, finally, break into the American market. They would begin by targeting a single state that had some 24 million privately owned cars, nearly as many as in all of Britain: California. And if he could convince Annette, they would fly out together and kick-start things themselves.

By the spring of 1975, when they made the first of a series of visits that year, some of the spadework had already been done. John Hall, Haynes's first full-time salesman in the late-1960s, was sent out to run the embryonic US business. He had found warehousing space. US versions of a number of the manuals were soon being shipped out to California every few weeks, and the operation had actually begun to turn a small profit.

But no amount of spadework could entirely shield their young children from the effect of their transatlantic commuting. They would, of course, do all that they could to cushion the effect. They would take Chris with them. He was not yet even four. And J, who had just turned eight, was quite content to move to a prep school near Yeovil as a full boarder. Yet Marc's situation was more complicated. Though he'd been happy at his primary school, once he turned seven there was no day school in the area that could accommodate a child with his disabilities. The nearest option was a special-needs school an hour away in Taunton, which accepted him as a five-day boarder. Marc didn't so much mind the boarding: Annette would drive him there early each Monday, return at the end of the week, and pick him up at noon every Wednesday, when there was only a half-day of classes. What upset and unsettled him was the entirely new school environment: the jolt of leaving his mainstream primary for a school explicitly aimed at children with special needs.

In the run-up to their first LA trip, preparations for their absence were put in place. Since their original live-in housekeeper had left, they hired a couple named Gordon and Gwyneth Gooding to tend to household chores and help with childcare. They moved into the barn, which was no longer home to the printing operation and had been fixed up as comfortable living quarters. While Annette was away, they took over getting Marc to and from school, and cared for him at Camway over the weekends.

Still, it was not easy. In a period of twelve months, she and John flew back and forth five times. By mid-1976, with his

American company growing but not yet really taking off, John convinced himself – and, gradually, Annette as well – that the only way to make that happen would be to move to California, at least for a year or so. Though Annette was already taking on a role on the business side, she had only one condition. She and John agreed that she, and John when he could, would fly back for every half-term school holiday. On the longer breaks – Easter, summer holiday and Christmas – they'd have the children fly out to LA. Ether way, *all* the holidays would be spent as a family.

On their last commuting trip to California, they'd found – and bought – a house. It was a large, recently built, two-storey family home – four bedrooms, three bathrooms, more than 3,000 square feet. To John's delight, it also had *three* garages, two of which would before long be occupied, since John decided to take his Jaguar E-Type along from England, and within weeks had also purchased a Ford Mustang. Perhaps best of all, the property was perched on a hill, with a commanding view of the San Fernando valley.

Chris thrived at a local kindergarten. He was also inevitably included in some of the more exotic business excursions that John and Annette found themselves taking in order to find a way to establish a significant presence in the US. The first came only weeks after their arrival: a trip to Las Vegas for a major trade exhibition, during which the three of them bedded down at the Stardust Hotel on the strip.

Annette took to the States as well: the bustle, the energy, the unfamiliarly wide-open spaces. Not to mention the weather. As in the early days at Camway, she played an active part in John's newly accelerated efforts to bring Haynes Manuals to a new, and potentially enormous, audience, eventually taking charge of making sure the right manuals, in the required quantities, were getting shipped out from Sparkford.

They faced major competition in the States, from two companies in particular: Clymer and Chilton. But just as John had managed to distinguish his manuals from Autobooks in Britain, he was determined to carve out a profitable area of his own in the US. The niche was obvious to him. The US companies' manuals dealt almost exclusively with American-made cars. Haynes not only *could* provide its uniquely down-to-earth manuals for British makes. He already had a range of titles that, with editorial tweaks, could be marketed for American owners. He'd done manuals on other popular European imports as well: from Volkswagens to Porsches. And he had an especially large head start on the American companies in another growing market for American car-buyers: the imported Japanese models.

That part of John's campaign – the search for a niche presence – bore fruit pretty quickly. They were soon selling tens of thousands of manuals – on British, European and Japanese imports – each month. They'd clearly also tapped into many Americans' view of high-performance European cars, in particular, as alluringly exotic – a bit like Cuban cigars for smokers. Proof positive came shortly after they moved to LA, when sales of the Haynes manual on the Porsche 911 outstripped, by some distance, the number of Porsches that were actually being sold there.

But it was still only a niche, and for John, it was still not enough. True success in the US could come only by entering the turf that, for years, had been dominated by the two main American companies. In other words, he'd have to create manuals on American cars. At this point, they had no facilities in the US for giving these makes the Haynes treatment. Even in the UK operation, John himself had largely moved on from the process of taking the cars apart and putting them back together.

The solution turned out to be an unorthodox example of US–British cooperation. The team in Sparkford began approaching the commanders of American military bases. A swap arrangement was put in place. Haynes's mechanics would ask for a particular car model. The soldier or officer who owned it would then be offered a full tear-down, service and comprehensive repair of anything found amiss, with the promise that it would be returned good as new in a couple of weeks, cost-free. He'd also be given one of Haynes's company cars – an Audi – for the duration.

The US business was now growing. About six months after the move to LA, a new, larger base – with warehousing and offices – was set up in Newbury Park, north-west of the city. It would be a full decade before John's grand vision succeeded, and Haynes could truly claim to a major player on the US motor-publishing landscape. But even at this stage, John had every reason to feel confident that he'd get there. Barely a year after the move to California, one of the American rivals, Clymer, clearly had taken notice of him. It filed an 'anti-dumping' petition against Haynes, alleging that John was selling his manuals at less than what it cost to produce them. For a while it was a cause for real concern, and repeated huddling with lawyers, but it was ultimately dismissed.

But John Haynes – to borrow a line from American cinema, which his commuting family, especially J, were coming to love – was obviously not in Kansas anymore. He'd become an international businessman. He made no pretence at being a titan: a Rockefeller, a Henry Ford, or, for that matter, a William Morris. But he did take pride in the extraordinary growth of the little business he'd set about constructing when he first arrived from MoD Harrogate with his wife, their infant child and their meagre possessions in a beat-up Bedford Van. It was only partly in jest that he chose the paint jobs for the small fleet of delivery vans now being used to help with distribution back in the UK. 'Haynes Publishing Group,' the side panels read, 'Leeds … Sparkford … Los Angeles.'

In John's mind, the next step was the one that he'd begun discussing at the start of the decade with the finance experts at

Singer & Friedlander: making Haynes a public company, listed on London's stock exchange.

Even in Los Angeles, he never ceased pressing for a way to make that happen. In a quality that proved alternately endearing, inspiring, frustrating and sometimes maddening to those around him, John was not so much a traditional business owner as a catalyst and a visionary. He was endlessly gripped by the attraction of finding some new way to expand or accelerate what the company was doing. The role of others – his accountant, his lawyer, occasionally other managers, at times Annette, or in this case all of the above – was to provide a brake. Or at times, a simple reality check. Haynes's business success would never have been possible without both sides of this process.

Now, the reality was that Britain was in a rolling economic and political crisis. The effects of the oil embargo had eased somewhat, but the public finances were in a mess. In fact, just a few months before John and Annette moved to LA in 1976, with the value of the pound at a record low, the government of Labour Party Prime Minister Jim Callaghan had had to go in hand to the International Monetary Fund for a bailout loan of nearly four billion dollars. That settled things for a while, but did nothing much to quell rising internal divisions inside Labour, and increasing pressure from the trade unions. Still, John remained in contact with the head of the merchant bank. And neither the day-to-day demands of the US business – nor even the periodic reunions with J and Marc, including memorable excursions to Disneyland and drives up to the California coast – could entirely quash his appetite for going ahead with the flotation.

Fortunately, for those around him counselling caution, John had deep misgivings about placing a major chunk of his company's equity on the market. He had built Haynes Publishing, through all the zigs and zags since producing the first true Haynes manual on the trestle table in the spare bedroom of their Aden apartment, on his, and Annette's, grit and determination. It was a family business; despite the allure of taking it public, he was set on keeping it that way. He was equally clear that he would remain its driving force. 'I have yet to meet a man,' he told a friend at the time, 'who is still involved with his company, who has lost control, and remained happy.'

By 1978, with John and Annette still travelling to LA but resettled back in Camway, that concern, at least, became moot. The London Stock Exchange lowered the minimum equity requirement for a public placement, meaning that John could limit the stock placement to 25% of the company's value. Still, there remained a huge amount of preparatory work to be done with Singer & Friedlander. Over the next year, they strategised over precisely how, and when, to go ahead with the share issue, and at what price to offer the shares. The political and economic winds, too, seemed to be changing. Though there was still considerable uncertainty on the markets, Britain's general election in May 1979, on the heels of a spate of public-sector strikes, had replaced Jim Callaghan's Labour government with an unapologetically free-market Conservative one led by Margaret Thatcher.

In late November 1979, in tandem with Singer & Friedlander's managing director, Panton Corbett, Haynes formally issued the prospectus for the company's market flotation. In setting the minimum offer price for the million-and-a-quarter shares being put out for public tender, John had accepted Corbett's advice to scale back his initial figure of £1.20. Instead, they'd be offering them at a minimum of 95p. Even that would be asking the public, in effect, to bet on the still-unrealised future of all that Haynes had accomplished so far. The so-called 'net asset value' of the existing company, laid out in the prospectus, was 27p.

Still, if John was apprehensive as the three-day window for applications from the public opened in early December, he managed almost faultlessly to hide his nerves, sharing them

only with Annette. On the day that the offer closed, the two
of them travelled up to London with the other three members
of the company's board: Frank Day, their managing director;
John's personal accountant, David Suter; and a dapper,
white-haired gentleman listed, for the purposes of the stock
placement, as company secretary. At age 82, Harold Haynes,
John's father, had the distinction of being the oldest listed
company secretary in the land. As soon as they entered the
room set aside by Panton Corbett, John beamed and held
Annette close to savour the moment. In front of them, nearly
two dozen clerks were sorting through thousands of share
applications. By the time the calculations were over, Corbett
informed them that there had been more than thirteen times
the number of responses – each with a cheque – needed to
sell the 25% of the company they'd put out to tender. Some
of the offers were for the minimum: 95p. But others were for
more. Some were as high as £1.70. Once the cheques from the
unsuccessful applicants were returned, the new minimum
share price was announced: exactly the £1.20 John had
hoped for.

And a total of £1.5 million was now injected into the business
he'd begun building from scratch, part-time, while still in the
air force.

That should have lent a new kind of ballast to the company,
and modulated the breakneck pace at which John himself had
moved in the years leading up to the flotation. And to some
extent, both those things did happen. One force for steadiness
and stability was his brother, David. Now fully qualified as a
chartered secretary and winding down his second stint in the
RAF, he'd assumed an informal role alongside the nominal
company secretary – their father, Harold – even before the stock
placement. In 1981, after leaving the air force, he became Haynes
Publishing's company secretary. He became a steadying presence

or, as another of the top executives described it, an 'important counterpoint to John's exuberance'.

There were other reconnections with family as well. Harold and Vi, still in fairly good health but slowed by age, moved into a small, bungalow-style home just around the corner from Camway. And with the death of Annette's stepfather, her mother, Dee, to whom she'd always been close, became an even more frequent visitor. The presence of all three was not only a source of comfort for John and Annette, but for the children as well, especially Marc. Dee's visits were also an occasion of almost invariable mirth for Annette and John, as they watched the balletic interactions among their parents. Dee was still an attractive, vivacious, self-confident woman, all qualities Annette had inherited in full measure. She was also the near-diametric opposite of Vi. They did like each other, and they shared a fundamental kindness. But Dee shamelessly enjoyed flirting with Harold, who was equally incapable of not enjoying the attention. Vi – heroically, stoically – looked on, as if to say: let the children have their little games.

But even with the infusion of new capital, and a more formal management structure in place, John's instinct was to carry on running Haynes Publishing as he'd always done. It was, in his mind, still same business. His business. He'd nurtured and expanded it not so much through any formal strategy, as with intuition and improvisation: seeing opportunities, sizing them up, and if they made sense, grabbing them and moving on to the next one. There was a problem with that now. As a listed company, Haynes not only had to answer to shareholders, he also had to abide by a web of specific rules and regulations applied to any business on the stock exchange.

The first reality check had actually come right before the flotation. It involved Leeds, one of the trio of names on the side of John's delivery vans. The old tobacco warehouse was now quite literally straining at the seams. The wooden floors had not been designed for the weight of the manuals and other books sent out for distribution around the north of England. Yet right across the street, a large and more solidly constructed building, was coming on the market. It had been used by the Yorkshire company Associated Dairies, part of the 1960s merger to form Asda, to store the huge quantities of milk it delivered by float around the city. Moving the Haynes warehouse operation there was straightforward. But John couldn't help noticing that the depot also included a large car park. Nor could he help thinking: there's an opportunity there. He could use part of the area to rent out to a couple of small, start-up enterprises, as a kind of Haynes Publishing business park. Singer & Friedlander did manage to talk him out of that. He was, after all, about to issue the first shares in a *publishing* company. This kind of *non*-publishing excursion was not going to help. Still, John was undaunted. As a fall-back, he asked why he couldn't just buy the car park on his own, as a personal investment? Which is what he did.

Even that was not completely without consequence. At the first AGM after the stock-exchange listing, one shareholder noticed John's personal interest in the car park. He had, in fact, played things completely by the book. It was a genuinely arms-length transaction, involving no resources from the company. Still, the questioner kept pressing for details: how much profit was he making from this side-investment, and wasn't that money that the *company* could have made?

But John had far grander designs, in any case. They didn't involve side-deals, or car parks. His focus was on using the company's new resources not just to expand further in Britain; he would build on the foundations that he and Annette had laid down in Los Angeles, and make Haynes a – *the*, if all went to plan – major publishing player in the largest single car market in the world.

*Chapter Ten*

# FLOATING FREE

It would prove to be a long haul. And despite the new cash and new ambitions, it is hard to imagine how things could have started worse.

For Margaret Thatcher, as for John Haynes, 1979 had marked a new beginning. She, of course, was running a country, not a company. But she had entered 10 Downing Street with an equally firm sense of what she wanted to achieve. Much of it was influenced by the free-market doctrines of the American economist Milton Friedman. She wanted to get the country moving again, essentially by undoing the nationalisations of the post-Second World War Labour government, deregulating markets and reining in the power of the trade unions. And over time, admired and reviled in equal measure, depending on which side of the ideological fence you were on, she managed to accomplish all three.

But not immediately. She inherited a Britain beset by inflation and recession, and still reeling from the so-called Winter of Discontent: a rash of strikes a year earlier that had involved not just industry but a range of services from refuse-collection to grave-digging.

So, as Haynes embarked on his own new beginning, inflation remained high, as did the value of the British pound against the dollar. Industrial action by one of the print unions, the

National Graphical Association, cut production by something like 150,000 manuals. Ahead of the stock-market flotation, John had told Annette that only four things worried him: 'the dollar going the wrong way, strikes, sales slowing down because of the economic situation, or a lack of stock.' Now, he'd hit the trifecta. And that wasn't all. A few months later, fire engulfed one of the outbuildings on the expanded site in Sparkford, causing about £50,000 in damage. At least there were no books there, just cardboard packaging. And he had learned the lesson from the fire at his garage warehouse in Cambridge twenty years earlier: he did have insurance. Still, it was hardly an ideal beginning.

Nor was he the only one worried. Returning from one of their trips to California early in 1980, he and Annette were met by a familiar figure at the airport: Panton Corbett of Singer & Friedlander. He, as Annette recalls, was also deeply unsettled.

John was undaunted, however. And while he continued periodically to jet off to Los Angeles to try to build up the business there, he had more than enough to preoccupy him closer to home. The stock-market listing had made not only Haynes Publishing, but John too, financially secure. As majority shareholders, he and Annette were wealthier than either of them could have envisaged. This showed no signs of changing who they were: neither of them harboured some pent-up desire for yachts or private jets or Caribbean islands. But it was liberating. It widened John's horizons, both for his business and his family.

At work, the stock flotation showed no signs of constraining his idiosyncratic management strategy – the high-octane mix of intuition and improvisation. Instead, it seemed to supercharge it. It also rekindled his desire to be not just the leading publisher of motor manuals, but a true *book* publisher. Within the space of a few years, he made a whole series of new acquisitions. He bought the small, well-respected Oxford Illustrated Press. The brainchild of a woman named Jane Marshall, who joined

Haynes, it was known for a series of glossy car histories, but also produced a list of non-motoring titles on topics ranging from photography to mountain climbing. Next, he acquired the motoring titles of a publisher called Gentry Books. Then, a clutch of transport publications from Penguin – but not 'transport' as in cars. Most of them dealt with military transport. Finally, he purchased another Oxford publisher that was one of the world's leading specialists in railway books. There was only one dud: a venture into magazine publishing. He backed a new, high-end monthly called *Automobile Sport*, which, since he had no knowledge of the magazine-advertising market, quietly folded after just a few issues.

Still, he never lost sight of the core of the business: the Haynes manuals. They had not only helped him build his business, they had *made* the business. They were what advertising executives would call its USP: its unique selling point. And amid the economic headwinds of the early 1980s, they remained the engine that kept Haynes Publishing growing. Not long after the share issue, Haynes had scored a major coup, complementing his arrangements with the network of cash-and-carry outlets in the north. He secured a distribution deal with Halfords, the nationwide group of several hundred stores retailing motoring parts and accessories, meaning tens of thousands of additional manuals sold each week. He'd been hoping for the Halfords link-up for years. In fact, shortly after he left the RAF – inspired, and daunted, by his visits to the Autobooks warehouse in Brighton – Annette and her mother had begun mischievously walking into random Halfords stores to ask for a Haynes manual. When, inevitably, they were told, sorry, never heard of them, but we have Autobooks, Annette would reply: 'The Haynes ones are way better. You should get them.' Now, finally, they had.

The greatest sense of satisfaction for John was what the Halfords arrangement signified. The manuals had become not merely desirable purchases for Britain's ever-growing population of automobile owners; for many, they were now staples, as much a must-have part of buying a car as its spare tyre. Some motor dealers were actually including the relevant Haynes manual when they made a sale. Mechanics, too, found them at least as useful as the manufacturers' own guides. For some enthusiasts, they were *aspirational* purchases, too: the Porsche 911 manuals were not the only ones bought not by actual owners, but by *would-be* owners. Even more striking, the manuals' now-familiar, formulaic approach had become part of Britain's culture, its very idiom. John would soon lose count of the times a satisfied customer, on realising who he was, would quote one of the manuals' trademark lines at him with a smile: 'Remember, *replacement is a reversal of the removal process*!'

*That* feeling – that kinship – was what he hoped, one day, to replicate with car-owners in the United States.

But the success of the stock offering also allowed him to focus his attention on his family. He was fiercely devoted to his three young sons, and what he wished for them was coloured by his own tea-plantation childhood in Ceylon. Now in his early forties, he could see that he'd been lucky. While his own father had enjoyed the status, and authority, conferred even by a waning British Empire, Harold had never accumulated any real wealth. A sizable chunk of his modest savings had gone toward sending John and David to Sutton Valence. There, John had never excelled in, nor much cared about, the academics or athletics. Yet he had nonetheless thrived. He'd been given *freedom*, with the support and friendship of key mentors, and that had encouraged and enabled him to pursue the unorthodox career path which had finally delivered his business success. Now, with personal resources far greater than Harold had ever enjoyed, he wanted his children to feel equally free to chart their own futures.

With his oldest son, J, having turned thirteen, John decided in 1981 to send him to Sutton Valence, with Chris following five years later. The decision at first startled Annette, since John had never voiced any particular nostalgia for his boarding school days. 'But he knew that he'd been able to do what he wanted to do there, and he said that he thought it would be good for the boys to make their own way, and to do what *they* wanted to do.'

Though John and Annette still periodically visited the US, their family life was also more settled again. The couple they'd hired as live-in support for the children in the 1970s had moved on around the time of the stock flotation. But through an advert in *The Lady* – the century-old magazine through whose weekly adverts generations of Britain's nannies had been hired – Annette now engaged a young couple from Oxford, Denis and Frances Morgan. They would remain for nearly thirty years, becoming very much part of the Haynes family.

Yet John also chose to use his new financial freedom for bricks and mortar. Camway had been – and still was – a lovely home. All three of their children had grown up there. It had also been part of the childhood of Haynes Publishing, when the barn had been converted into their printing base. There was a little shop just down the lane that had pretty much everything they needed, and a bakery up the hill in the village that delivered fresh loaves of bread to their door each morning. The setting, too, was lovely, with the river flowing alongside the back garden. But the main part of the house was centuries old. And the river, though it was pretty to look at, flooded once every few years.

He – and Annette too – had grown to love their home in California. It was spacious. It was in good nick, having been built barely a decade earlier. Above all, it was on high ground. Over breakfast, or as the sun set, they could sit and gaze out over the most wonderful view of the valley. Though John still enjoyed Camway, and wasn't going to move just for the sake of it, he wanted something similar for their home in Britain. For a couple of years, he and Annette spent the odd weekend looking for likely candidates, but without finding anything.

Then, early in 1982, he was away for a few days in California. Annette's mother had come to visit, and they spotted an advert in the local paper for an old home in a place called Bradford Abbas. It was a village not much bigger than West Camel, on the far side of Yeovil, and they drove out to take a look. The home was also larger than Camway, though it had clearly seen better days. It was called Coombe, from the Old English word for a hillside. From the outside, as Annette described it to John when he returned, it looked like a 'Victorian Gothic monstrosity'. But the first thing she'd seen on entering the ground-floor hallway was a wide wooden staircase curling elegantly upstairs, and it was the real estate version of love at first sight. The property had been a working farm in the past, so there were dozens of acres stretching out from a glass-fronted sitting room at the rear of the bottom floor. And it was perched on high ground, with a beautiful view over the whole of the countryside. 'I think I might have found somewhere interesting,' she told John when he got back.

Within weeks, they had bought it. It did require work: redoing the ancient kitchen; rewiring and replumbing; adding central heating. Ensuring proper accommodation for the Morgans as well. All of that took time. But two years later, in August 1984, they moved in. J was back from Sutton Valence for the summer, Chris still a year from starting there, and they both loved the new home.

Marc did, too. But he would soon be parted from it.

His childhood health scare had long since passed. Not only had he survived infancy, he was now, against all odds, into his late teens. He seemed not so much oblivious to his disability, as determined – almost always cheerfully determined – to pretend it simply didn't exist. Even though he'd been confined

*Above* Courier service: John racing his Elva Courier
~~at~~ Silverstone during the summer of 1964, with
~~An~~nette (right) helping him refit the engine a few
~~mo~~nths earlier.

*Below* Surprise: the old Elva, which John had to
~~sell~~ before they headed out on RAF assignment to
~~Ad~~en, rediscovered in the late 1980s and presented by
~~An~~nette as a Christmas gift.

Above *Birth of an idea: John (right) and his RAF friend in Aden, David Hyland, hauling the engine of David's Austin Healey Sprite up the four flights of sta to the Haynes flat to begin disassembling, repairing ( then reassembling it, with John photographing every step and recording the details. The result would be th first true Haynes Motor Manual.*

Left *Shades of a Rockstar: John with newlywed David Hyland and his wife, Delores, in Aden.*

Below *Home comforts: the photograph of Annette and the MGA taken on their honeymoon that John kept in his wallet throughout his life.*

*Above* Business beginnings: John's brother, David, with colleagues John Hall and Margaret Ibbotson at the Motorists Bookshop, which shared space with the networks David set up in Lower Odcombe, Somerset, as the Haynes Publishing business took shape.

*Right* Delivery vehicle: Annette in the Triumph TR4 which she and John sometimes used for book deliveries in the early stages of the business.

*Below left* Growing up: John, with colleague John Hall (background), son J and apprentice John Warry taking delivery of paper for the printing operation after moving it into the reconditioned barn at Camway, the home they purchased in the Somerset village of West Camel.

*Right* Home of Haynes: the disused creamery in Sparkford, Somerset, that John purchased in the early 1970s as a base to bring together all the strands of his motor manual operation – and which would remain Haynes Publishing headquarters for the rest of his life.

JJ AND MARC IN SPAIN c̄ DADDY AND MUMMY

*Above* Family time: John and Annette with their young son J and infant Marc on holiday in Spain.

*Left* New arrival: returning home to Camway with their third child, Chris, with John showing the signs of his brief experiment with amphetamine-based diet pills.

*Below* Rite of passage: J and Marc at their joint christening in the summer of 1968.

*above California dreaming: the home near Los Angeles – with three garages, to John's particular delight, and a commanding view of the San Fernando Valley – that he purchased in the mid-1970s with a view to building up Haynes Publishing's business in the United States.*

*above right Beach outing: with all three sons at the Malibu Beach Club.*

*right Hilltop: with son J on Castle Peak in West Hills, near LA, during the Easter holiday in 1977.*

*right American roots: John, with the briefcase that travelled with him everywhere, outside Los Angeles International Airport on his first trip to LA. Followed two years later with Annette and their youngest son, Chris.*

*below Boxing days: taking delivery of manuals from the UK at the Haynes LA warehouse in the first years of the US operation, before printing shifted to a dedicated facility in Nashville.*

**Above** *Camway jubilee: John and Annette at a West Camel village celebration of the Queen's Silver Jubilee in 1977 with (l-to-r) Annette's stepfather, R mother Dee, and Dee's father, Daniel Davies.*

**Left** *Family trio: Marc, Chris and J in a childhood portrait Annette presented John for their 25th wedding anniversary.*

**Below** *First Rolls: with the family beside John's fir Rolls-Royce, a Phantom II.*

*Above Rollsing on: with the Phantom and his next two additions to his Rolls-Royce collection – a Corniche and 20/25 Drophead.*

*Below Flotation celebration: the Haynes board days before the company was floated on the stock exchange in 1979 (l-to-r): Neville Sanders; John's father, Harold, Frank Day, John, David Suter and Annette.*

**Above** *Speed pairing: John with world land-speed recordholder Richard Noble at the formal opening of the motor museum in 1985.*

**Below** *Silver celebration: the Haynes family togeth[er] in June 1988, on the 25th anniversary of John's a[nd] Annette's wedding.*

to a wheelchair, there was almost nothing that J and Chris got up to which Marc could see any reason not to join: even, on one memorable occasion when he was about eight, going 'stickleback-tickling' on the bank of the river behind Camway – trying to coax the little fish into jam jars – only to tumble out of his wheelchair into a patch of stinging nettles.

But he *was* disabled. He'd had a number of procedures over the years to strengthen his spine, and to address the myriad other effects of his condition.

In 1985, around the time of his seventeenth birthday, surgeons at Nuffield Hospital in Oxford had inserted a number of metal struts to help stabilise his spine. And just two and a half years later, his doctors felt the need to deal with another condition that could no longer be finessed by half-measures. He had developed a sinus – basically a hole – in his groin. They'd tried a number of treatments, most recently using a suction pump to try to keep it from getting worse, but they were concerned it might deepen and eventually rupture the main, femoral artery in his thigh. So they had him admitted to one of the country's top spinal-injury units, at Stoke Mandeville Hospital in Aylesbury. It was north-west of London, some 140 miles away. The doctors there tried a host of different treatments, but none of them worked. Marc would end up remaining there for nearly seven months, and Annette moved full-time to be with him. In the end, the doctors could think of only one way of minimising the risk of future complications: they removed part of one of his thighs, and reattached what remained in order to close up the space in his groin area.

John never permitted his worries about his son's condition to show. Friends put this down to not wanting to further burden his son, and that was part of it, but only part. And, oddly enough, it was an act of solicitude that this particular disabled teenager may not have needed. Even the trials of his latest operation seemed to barely faze him. At one of the still-frequent parties

John and Annette hosted after his return, John's brother, David, noticed a half-dozen teenage girls, laughing loudly, in a rough circle in the back garden. At its centre was Marc, doing what would soon become something of a party trick, now that he had only one thigh. He had lifted the thigh-less leg and positioned it, like an acrobat or a yogi, behind his neck.

Yet perhaps the main reasons for John's absence of much visible concern about Marc's condition came from inside John himself. Like his son, he appeared to believe, or at least hope, that ignoring the effects of his disability might strip them of their power. And just as his pub-night bonhomie had always masked a quieter, pensive, private person, the pain that John felt, because of the pain Marc had had to endure, was something that, with very rare exceptions, he kept inside.

But there was one increasingly important part of his life in which John did wear his feelings – a wide-eyed, almost adolescent joy – on his sleeve. And that, too, had roots going all the way back to the hilltop plantation in Ceylon.

It had to do with cars – of course, it did – but not just buying them to drive them, or even race them. Even as a small child, John was drawn to automobiles not just because of what was inside them, what they could do, how fast they could move – although all of that intrigued him. The first connection was with their *form*, and the ways in which a myriad of visionaries and manufacturers had married function with beauty. He had gazed in covetous wonder at the photos of early Fords and other American cars in his father's glossy magazines. He'd eagerly unwrapped his Christmas gift a few years later, and spent weeks, attentive to every detail, as he built a tiny wooden likeness of a sleek Jaguar. And, along with his little brother David, he'd avidly collected, and tenderly cared for, Dinky Toy replicas of dozens of other America, British and continental models.

His adult Dinky Toy period – though he'd never have seen it, much less described it, that way – began at the end of the

1960s, not long after he'd left the RAF and moved with Annette to Somerset. They had two young children then: J was not even two and Marc, barely one, was still not showing any signs of disability. It was a delightful spring day, and John drove north toward Bristol for the first of what, in the years ahead, would become dozens upon dozens of automobile auctions. The car which he had his eye on was neither recent, nor sleek, nor quick – nothing like the AC Cobra he would purchase a few years later. It was forty years old. Since only one well-off woman had owned it for all those years, and only her chauffeur had driven it, it was in pristine condition. But the real significance of his choice was that it was an iconic creation of his early role model, William Morris: an Oxford Six Saloon.

Driving it back to Camway proved an adventure in itself. The first part went without incident. But when he got halfway up the steep incline taking him out of Bath onto the long stretch home to West Camel, the car stopped dead. It was the little engine that *couldn't*. For a minute or so, he was stumped, unsure whether to find someone to push him or tow him, or simply to turn back. Then, he recalled having read somewhere that the *reverse* gear in the old Oxfords provided more traction than the forward ones. He gently backed down to the bottom of the hill. Then he turned the Morris around, and went up backwards.

As the pace of the auctions, and the purchases, accelerated, John was drawn to a number of other of Morris's classic creations, including a 1917 Morris Cowley and a 1955 Morris Minor convertible. In a nod to his first Sutton Valence step towards a career centred around automobiles, he also bought a 1934 Austin Seven. But his tastes were eclectic. Sometimes he was attracted by sleekness and speed. Sometimes, by the special place a model occupied in automotive history. Or by refinement, luxury. So he bought a powerful Chevy Corvette, a TVR Tuscan, a Lotus and a Porsche. And, of course, the AC

Cobra. He collected MGs and Aston Martins and Mercedes; a clutch of Jaguars; a Lincoln Continental Town Car; and an old 1905 Daimler with a detachable top. He had a particular soft spot for Rolls-Royces.

Never did he seem more serenely happy than when locating, purchasing, caring for, and finally driving one of his steadily growing collection. J would particularly remember one rainy afternoon in the early 1980s when the whole family piled into one of his father's favourite acquisitions: a 1971 Rolls-Royce Corniche convertible, one of the very first produced in a line that would continue until the mid-1990s. They headed south-west into Devon. Their destination was a former RAF airfield outside the village of Dunkeswell. As Annette, Chris and Marc looked on, he turned to J and said: 'Come on, let's hop in. Get behind the wheel and we'll take it for a spin.' J was by now fifteen years old. So unlike when he'd shared John's maiden drive in the AC Cobra a decade earlier, he could at least see over the dash. But he'd never driven a car before, and though the gear-shift wasn't a problem, since it was an automatic, he built his speed up gradually, and levelled out at barely 30 miles an hour. 'Come on,' John said, smiling. 'Can't you go a bit faster?' So J did. Then, suddenly, the car hit a watery pothole and the right front hubcap went chuntering off to the side. Mortified, J pumped on the brake and slowed the Rolls to a halt.

John simply laughed. 'We'd better go out and find the hubcap,' he said. As they did so, it was clear that the exhaust was damaged as well. But before J could gather his wits, much less apologise, his father said: 'Look, there is no way you could have seen that pothole. It was an accident. Accidents happen.'

They did indeed, and John himself was not immune. Back in 1973, in the very early stages of discussing his eventual purchase of the Oxford Illustrated Press, he'd driven up in one of his most distinctive automotive possessions, a lilac-coloured Jaguar saloon, to speak with the publisher's owner. Returning home in the evening, he came to a stop at a T-junction. As he later confessed to Annette, he'd been 'distracted' when an attractive woman in a mini-skirt stepped off the kerb, and he had begun to inch the car forward – only to be hit hard by an oncoming car. This wasn't just an errant hubcap. It was clear that the Jag was going to need a few months' attention before it could get back on the road. John's response – he *could* be a bit flash at times, was how Annette remembers it – was to go straight out and buy a brand-new V12 Jaguar E-Type.

After J's more minor mishap in Devon, John soon got the Corniche fixed up again. He had also quickened the pace of his acquisitions: subscribing to classic-car magazines, seeking out auctions, and adding to his collection. Which one of the cars he chose to drive, though he did develop firm favourites, depended on his mood, where he was driving, sometimes on the weather. But since he now had nearly thirty of them, there was no way that Camway, or even the much larger property in Bradford Abbas, could accommodate them all. Some were parked at Sparkford or at other of Haynes's company facilities. Others were in sheds or lock-ups. Some were in friends' garages.

Sooner or later, he figured, he'd find a way to bring most, if not all, of them together in a single location. But when he woke one sunny Saturday morning in Coombe with a hankering to set out in one of his Jaguars, he realised he'd simply forgotten where he'd stowed it. For some time, he had been playing with the idea of finding somewhere not just to keep all of the cars but to formalise what was now increasingly obvious not just to him but everyone around him: these weren't just the random purchases of an especially avid car-lover. John had become a car-*collector*. They were a collection, and what he really needed was a place not just to park them, but exhibit them.

He had another concern, too, which had been nagging at him for a couple of years, since the death of a good friend, and fellow car-enthusiast, who he and Annette had met during their time in California. He, too, had amassed several dozen classic cars. But after he passed away, the need for his estate to cover the taxes, meant that the collection was broken up. John had begun to notice that a lot of the cars he saw when he went to the auctions were also part of estates that were being sold. Though still in his forties, and planning to stick around for a good few years yet, he was determined to ensure that *his* car collection would outlive him.

*How* he ended up doing that was down to the two men he asked for advice: his accountant David Suter, and his lawyer, Neville Sanders. Why not, they asked, set up a charitable trust, and donate all the cars you've been collecting to the trust?

For Suter, one obvious advantage was financial: there would, even now, be a significant tax saving. John did pay attention to such things. One attraction of the nearly eighteen months he and Annette had spent in Los Angeles, for instance, was the comparatively steep taxation rates in late-1970s Britain. It wasn't that he objected to paying taxes. He sought none of the corporate, or offshore, loopholes which attracted many other well-off business figures. Yet he was quite open to saving on his tax bill through perfectly legal, widely recognised means of lowering what he owed to the Revenue. Still, importantly, he never in all his business life made a decision simply *in order* to get such a benefit. As Annette points out, 'He was certain the only way we would ever establish the company in America was for us to be there for a stretch of time. We'd *tried* working through local companies or agents, and we were getting nowhere. So we were going to go there anyway.' It was the same thing with the idea of what to do with the cars. He wouldn't do it simply to save on his present tax bill, as Suter well knew. It was the other argument he made which ultimately held sway, and answered John's real concern: that if he gave the cars to a trust, the collection would outlive him. As Suter put it, 'They'll still be there after you're gone.'

Still, he had his misgivings. Even though he'd be giving the cars to the trust, he *would* be parting ways with them, and that wasn't easy. In fact, he did keep several of his favourites back, including the AC Cobra, a newly acquired Ferrari Berlinetta Boxer, and his ever-present Jaguar XK150. Even then, as he recounted to his speed-trial friend AJ Jeans, his 'hand hovered for a long time' before he signed on to the arrangement. Yet the more he thought about it, the more he was attracted to the idea of the trust, no doubt in part because it had echoes of the earlier, if undeniably wealthier, motoring pioneer whom he'd long admired: William Morris. Morris's reputation had rested not just on his business accomplishments, but on the enormous scale of his philanthropy. John respected both. In his mind, donating the cars he was collecting – making them the core of more than just an exhibit, a *museum* – would be a way of making his own gift to those who came after him. As always, he was thinking big, imagining not just a few dozen, but ultimately maybe even a few hundred cars. But again in character, he wasn't about to let that keep him from starting small. And he did, by buying a disused sawmill in Sparkford in 1984 and then immediately interviewing candidates to help manage the museum.

The man he settled on was named Mike Penn. He had no experience at all of museums, except for occasionally having visited them. Until weeks earlier, he'd been a chief engineer in the British Navy's flying unit, the Fleet Air Arm, where his role was to accompany combat helicopters on their operations.

He lived locally and also liked restoring classic cars as a hobby. It no doubt helped that his very first restoration project, like John's in Aden, had been an Austin-Healey Frogeye Sprite. But the clincher, for both John and Annette, who interviewed him as well, was that he was bright, engaging and brimmed, in equal measure, with energy and self-confidence. They told him he had the job on the same day he heard that he'd also got the one other post he'd applied for, and for which he *was* unquestionably qualified: as a senior instructor at Westland Helicopters. He chose the museum, though it did not yet exist.

But before long, it did. Dubbed the Sparkford Motor Museum, it was formally inaugurated in July 1985, with twenty-seven of John's cars, along with a pair of classic motorcycles. John – by now with a full beard – was flanked by a *bona fide* celebrity in the motoring world: Richard Noble, who had recently used his jet-propelled Thrust2 to break the land speed record in the Nevada desert.

His attendance, along with the presence of a gaggle of leading motoring journalists, was the first real sign that John Haynes's life was changing in another way as well: he was on his way to becoming something of a celebrity himself.

*Chapter Eleven*

# TAKE-OFF

The celebrity crept up on him, and for a while he didn't really notice, or at least give it much thought.

One reason was that, in addition to the museum project, Haynes was now – finally – poised to make his long-sought business breakthrough in America. Sales there had been building steadily through the early 1980s. Annette, who was in charge of getting the UK-printed manuals shipped, was dispatching as many as three 40-foot-long containers each week for distribution in the States. But their main American competitors – Clymer and Chilton – were still far, far outstripping them.

That started to change only about the time the museum was opened, with two newly promoted Haynes executives, Max Pearce and Eric Oakley, spearheading efforts to get the manuals into the three main US motor-accessory chain stores, something essential to any major expansion. The first major success came about a year after that, in December 1986, when Autozone, which had some 400 stores, agreed to sell Haynes manuals. Not long afterwards came Pep Boys, which had around 300 outlets. Finally, Chief Auto Parts, which had long been Clymer's key outlet, agreed to take on the Haynes titles. All that would have been encouraging enough. But Clymer's response was even more significant: it suddenly decided to get out of the car-manual business altogether, in effect leaving

Chilton, though still number one by some distance, as Haynes's only major competitor.

These were heady days. With Clymer out of the way, sales began to rise more strongly. And Chilton's books were quite different from John Haynes's manuals. They tended to be general takes on the major car companies' offerings, rather than model-specific, step-by-step guides. John felt it was now time to make a new push forward, especially with the Newbury Park office-and-warehouse complex he'd opened when he and Annette had decamped to Los Angeles a decade earlier at full capacity. Rather than expand, or replace, his California base, it was decided to open an entirely new warehouse and shipping facility, an 'eastern distribution centre', on the other side of the country.

They settled on Nashville, in Tennessee, a choice prompted initially by the fact that more than two-thirds of Americans lived within a 1,000-mile radius of the city. That meant that pretty much all bulk orders could be delivered overnight. But there was another attraction: the election, in 1987, of a modernising state governor named Ned McWherter, with whom John and Annette struck up a warm personal relationship. McWherter not only saw the Haynes investment in itself as good for Tennessee, but, with John's wholehearted encouragement, he also viewed it as a potential example for other British or European firms – a vision, though ultimately unfulfilled, which even led for a time to non-stop commercial flights between Nashville and Heathrow.

The launch of the Nashville complex, along with Clymer's retreat, represented a turning point. By the end of the 1980s, Haynes would control a solid, and still-growing, 40% of the motor-manual market in the US. And crucially – since this, after all, was the initial impetus for John to tap into the world's largest automobile market – US revenues seemed on a path towards equalling, and very probably outpacing, Haynes's UK operation.

John Haynes, who had so wanted, a couple of decades earlier, to stake his claim as a successful *London* publisher, was now on his way to becoming a successful *international* publisher. That distinction mattered, and it goes a long way toward explaining his uneasy relationship with the public recognition he was beginning to receive.

When he and Annette would go to publishing events in the capital, John would often be asked where Haynes Publishing was based, often inevitably triggering looks of pure astonishment. 'Somerset? *Sparkford?*' he'd be asked. 'What are you doing down *there?*' John had a number of ready replies: good printing facilities; space to expand; good road connections. But the truth was that he simply liked it there. London's glitter, its energy and pace, had seemed attractive when he'd first moved there, in his early twenties, after returning from his RAF posting in Germany. But in fact, he was much better suited to the quieter, more open spaces of Somerset. He was, at heart, provincial.

Even there, as a big fish in a decidedly smaller pond, he was never fully at ease as a public figure. Among friends and family – the latter category increasingly including his employees and *their* families – he did enjoy being the centre of attention. His clubbing and dancing days were now largely behind him, but he and Annette regularly entertained at Coombe, their hilltop home in Bradford Abbas. They'd host an especially large party a few days before Christmas. The star turn, not just for the kids, was John's grand entry as Father Christmas, a role for which his expanding girth and greying beard made him a natural.

But the wider, more public attention at first simply surprised him. In the weeks running up to the opening of the motor museum, Mike Penn, who was every bit as ambitious for the new project as John himself, pressed for it to be called the *Haynes* Motor Museum rather than the Sparkford Museum, arguing that the Haynes name would confer instant credibility and cachet with the motoring public. John rejected the idea. It somehow didn't feel right. It took several years for Penn and others to bring him around, and even then he was reluctant, agreeing at first only to rename it the Haynes Sparkford Museum. Only later did he acquiesce to dropping the 'Sparkford'.

His first brush with genuine, top-table exposure had a similar note of awkwardness about it. Among the business associates who had become personal friends over the years, he was especially fond of the train of bank managers who had run the local Barclays branch. Although he was now the chairman of a listed company with millions of pounds in turnover, he'd never lost the habit, from his first, hand-to-mouth days in Somerset, of daily visits to the bank, where he'd invariably check the balance, withdraw a few crisp bills for the day's spending money, and chat for a few minutes. In the autumn of 1988, the branch manager, Geoff Bullevant, draped a hand around his shoulder and confided that Barclays had been enlisted to sponsor a dinner to help raise money for British Olympic athletes. He'd immediately thought of John, he said, as a leading figure in the area's business community. Not only did he hope he could count on John and Annette to attend, but he proposed to seat John at the head table alongside the guest of honour: former Olympian, not to mention the daughter of the queen, Princess Anne.

John was, in his brother David's words, 'tickled pink'. He was also a bit overwhelmed, and not a bit nervous in the run-up to the dinner, held at Westland's headquarters in Yeovil. As promised, he was seated to the right of Princess Anne. On her other side was the region's titular royal representative, the Lord Lieutenant of Somerset. The first half hour of the dinner was excruciating for John. Unschooled in, and unused to, the choreography of such royal visits, he sat mortified as the princess chatted exclusively with the lord lieutenant. She completely ignored him. Yet then, as if a switch had suddenly been tripped, she turned to John with equal focus and engaged him in clearly well-briefed conversation about Somerset, about his family, and about the famous Haynes motor manuals.

He was, Annette recalled, 'quite chuffed'. And no less so when, not long afterwards, the two of them were invited by the American embassy to a London reception to celebrate British–American trade, along with their Tennessee friend and supporter, Governor McWherter and Britain's guest-of-honour, Her Majesty The Queen.

But he had very little time to savour his brush with royalty. In early December 1998, he and Annette were making their plans for their annual Christmas Party, starring John as Saint Nick, when they realised they would have to bring it forward by a few days. The shift was for the best of reasons. Marc had not only rebounded from his long stay at Stoke Mandeville, but, having obviously inherited not just John's determination but an ample dose of his charm, he had struck up a close relationship with one of the nurses caring for him. She'd since moved to Australia, and, in one of the frequent letters they had been writing each other, she had suggested he come out and spend a month with her there. He was due to fly out just a few days before Christmas.

John and Annette also brought forward another of their annual fixtures, a smaller pre-Christmas lunch for the immediate family, so that all three children could be there. Harold and Vi were there, too, of course. And while Annette's stepfather had passed away in the late 1970s, her mother, Dee, was the other guest.

As the lunch got under way, Vi seemed in especially good form. She rarely drank, but at Christmas she did traditionally indulge in a few sips of the locally popular, lightly alcoholic pear cider, Babycham. Even though she'd met up earlier with some friends in the village, and allowed herself a small sherry, she now had not one, but two little bottles of Babycham. She also had an extra helping of the turkey. But just as the meal was winding down, and Annette retreated to the kitchen to make coffee, she said that she felt a bit tired and withdrew to one of the big, comfortable chairs in Coombe's drawing room. The next thing Annette knew, Marc was wheeling himself into the kitchen. 'Mum, Grandma's not feeling very well. Gran's not feeling well,' he said. 'You should come see what's wrong.' She rushed back with him and saw John hovering over Vi, stroking her forehead. 'It's all right, Mother,' he was saying softly. 'It's all right.' But a few seconds later, she let out a long breath. Her head tilted to one side, and she died.

The week that followed was one of the most difficult in John's adult life. It was made no easier by having to bid a month's farewell to Marc at Heathrow a few days later, nor by the fact that, being John, he largely kept his grief inside. He got through it in part by focusing on the arrangement's for Vi's funeral – held, surrounded by family including her stepsisters, at the fourteenth-century Church of All Saints in West Camel. Over the days that followed, he tried to refocus all his energies on the business in which not he, but Vi too, had come to feel such pride. There, after all, things had rarely seemed brighter.

The problem – partly, but not only, for reasons beyond John's control – was that Haynes Publishing, too, would soon find itself in a sustained period of crisis. In fact, for a time, it seemed he might lose the company altogether.

*Chapter Twelve*

# CRISIS

For a while, the sun still shone brightly.

The children, each in their own way, were thriving. J, having spent a couple of years backpacking after going to Oxford Brookes University, was about to begin a stint as a graduate trainee with Haynes's bourgeoning US operation. Chris still had a couple of years left at boarding school. Marc, having returned from Australia, would be going on to university himself, to study business. But that was not all. In a turn of events that filled John with astonishment and pride in equal measure, Marc had fallen in love with the same kind of rakish sports cars as his father. In fact, he was determined not only to drive them, but race them. He had become good friends with a woman named Joy Rainey, a year or two older, who was a dwarf. She had nonetheless become a champion hill-climb racer in a specially adapted car. At her suggestion, Marc had joined a group of disabled drivers and had his own car fitted with hand controls. After competing in a few sprint competitions, he now wanted to engage in full-on motor racing.

He contacted the Royal Automobile Club, which was responsible for certifying drivers. 'Sorry,' the RAC official said, 'but given your condition, you can't, can you?' Marc replied that he wanted to, and insisted on taking the required driving test.

The driving part went fine, but he then had to pass a separate safety test, simulating an accident situation and requiring him to brake suddenly and get out of the car within a maximum of ten seconds. He prepared for it assiduously, collecting an assortment of pillows and sofa cushions and placing them on the driver's seat of his Nissan Silvia with a view to making it easier to propel himself out. He'd also bought himself a new racing helmet for the occasion. That, however, turned out to present a problem: with the ornately puffed-up seating arrangement, and his inability to bend his neck, it became clear there was no way he'd get his helmeted head under the car door frame. Marc didn't miss a beat. Turning to the RAC examiner, he said brightly: 'If you don't mind, I'm concerned I might damage my brand-new helmet. So can we dispense with that?' Absolutely, the man said; quite right. And so, placing it on the passenger's seat, Marc got in and, on cue, threw himself out of the car well within the allotted ten seconds. Smiling, he added: 'If my bum was on fire, I'd be out even quicker!' He passed.

John's and Annette's work life also purred along as before. They would get up around seven, have a leisurely breakfast, chatting and reading the morning paper and gazing out of the glass-fronted breakfast room at Coombe on the gently sloping countryside below. John would leave for the office around 8:30am, with Annette following an hour or so later, and they'd meet up for the regular train of company meetings with various of the executives, chaired by John: editorial, printing, distribution.

The major change was the museum. Its initial role was to provide a home for the disparate assortment of classic cars, sports cars and racing cars John had assembled over the years. But now, it had the effect of supercharging his desire to acquire yet more of them. He enlisted the ebullient former helicopter man who he'd hired to run the operation, Mike Penn, as a willing confederate. They were now subscribing to catalogues from all of the major motor-auction houses. John would leaf through each of them, putting a tick-mark beside four or five of the cars he might be interested in. Penn would then be dispatched a couple of days before each auction to go over every inch of each of the cars he'd selected, and to check out their ownership histories. He would write up a report for John to read the night before the auction. Then the two of them, very often with Annette as well, would go to the auction. Not always would John end up buying the cars he'd marked in the catalogue. Far more frequently, he would be smitten with another car altogether. Even if he *did* buy one of the automobiles that he'd sent Penn to check out, in the end it was almost always his own instinct – his on-the-day connection with a particular car – that won out. He was especially keen, for instance, on acquiring an Austin Healey 3000 at one of the sales. Penn had gone ahead to examine it, only to find that it came very close to defining the term 'lemon'. It had clearly been banged up. The undercarriage had been subjected to a decidedly inexpert series of patchwork repairs. All of this he'd duly alerted John to in his report. But on the day, John wanted it. And bought it. Annette, Penn recalled, was a much more rigorous judge of duds and bargains, though John did not always heed her auction advice either.

He was in his element: a man who loved cars now with free rein – and an undeniably charitable purpose – to act on his desires. His tastes were eclectic. At one auction, he came within a whisker of buying a British Army tank, before settling instead for a vintage 1928 Daimler. And he didn't give up the tank idea: he had Mike Penn source a Russian model from the old Yugoslav armed forces which, until it presented obvious health-and-safety issues, was briefly stationed outside the museum entrance, to the particular delight of child visitors.

On a number of occasions, John gave up drinking – the first time, not long after his mother's death, when he himself had gone for a routine physical exam at the GP. He was diagnosed with

Type 2 diabetes. The treatment the doctor recommended was non-intrusive: a once-a-day tablet, healthier diet and reduced alcohol consumption. So John did all three. But the second two lasted only a few months. John didn't really overeat. It was more that he had a few lifelong favourites he could never bring himself to abandon: especially a fondness for ice cream, which was rooted in childhood memories of Vi preparing her own on the tea plantation. As for the alcohol, he did go completely teetotal a few other times as well, before fully stopping nearly two decades later. 'But then we'd be out somewhere,' Annette recalls, 'and some idiot would always offer him a Scotch and soda. And that was it.'

Yet the auction outings were not limited to Britain. With the US business expanding, and J now apprenticing at the 'eastern' headquarters in Tennessee, John and Annette were travelling to the States at least three or four times a year. They would fly to Los Angeles, spend a week or so there, then come back through Nashville, where they'd combine business with a chance to reconnect with their eldest son, and then return to London. In Los Angeles, John had found a car-collecting dream. It was a cavernous warehouse on the outskirts of the city, run by a guy named Monty, who handled the private sale of classic American cars from the 1940s, '50s and '60s. The first full day of each visit to California, John would spend the morning in the office and then take a preliminary look at what Monty had on hand. Then he would spend the next week or so mulling over one of the especially enticing options, calculating what he thought it was worth, and return to try to seal the deal before their flight eastward to Tennessee, and then back home.

There was sometimes almost a kid-in-a-candy-shop feel to the visits to Monty's automobile treasure trove. On one trip, John's eyes fell on an old Model T, at which point he turned to Annette and said: 'Oh. That would be good for the museum, wouldn't it?' Monty, smiling, asked John whether he wanted to try it out – the equivalent of asking a young boy whether he'd like a bagful of chocolates. He and Annette got in, and drove it out into the enormous lot out in front. After a wide circuit of the area, he was happily heading toward the warehouse doorway when he turned to Annette and said: 'How do you stop it? I don't know how to stop it.' Fortunately, as he eased off the throttle, it halted, just in time, on its own.

Back home, however, was where trouble awaited in the early 1990s.

Haynes Publishing had grown into an incomparably larger, more complex and more profitable company than the one John had begun building more than 20 years earlier. It had hundreds of employees. Though still built around the car-manual idea born in an RAF flat in Aden, it had acquired a number of other small publishers and was producing a range of other books as well. No longer just a small family operation, it was a listed company, answerable to shareholders. It was managed and run with the help of a corps of experienced executives. Still, John and Annette remained on the board. John was its chairman and chief executive officer. Not every decision originated with him. But none of any consequence was, or could be, made without him. It was his energy and ebullience, his whirring ambition to accomplish more, and his vision that had built the company in the first place. They were still ultimately steering it, and especially with the increasingly buoyant outlook in the US, they gave every indication of steering it well.

His approach was never rooted in the kind of overarching strategy they teach in business school. It was more a set of rules and priorities he'd picked up along the way. Some of them, his brother David was convinced, dated from the broader life lessons their mother had sought to instil in them as children. Vi had learned a thing or two about how tough the world could be, and she preached the importance of building up a bulwark against unforeseen storms, above all by always living within one's means. She never read them Shakespeare before bedtime, but she did quote from the bard – one line in particular frequently enough that both John and David never forgot it: 'never a lender nor a borrower be.' John was always deeply uncomfortable borrowing money. In fact, Annette went further: 'John *hated* borrowing.' That was true even when, as they were just getting started in Somerset, he'd had little choice. They'd needed to take out a small mortgage to buy Camway, and on the other half of the stone house when it came on the market.

They'd had to borrow as well to purchase the printworks in Odcombe from David. But as soon as the business began making money, the first thing John Haynes did was to pay off all of them. Since the company was no longer just a small family business, Haynes Publishing, like other similarly sized enterprises, did, of course, sometimes borrow to fund specific investment or expansion. But John's gut discomfort over taking out loans never really went away.

And there was a corollary. Once John *did* own something, he was stubbornly reluctant to part with it. Not long before the stock-exchange flotation, for instance, he'd swapped the old, sagging tobacco warehouse in Leeds for the larger, sturdier former dairy warehouse across the way. The logical thing – or so it seemed to those around him focused on finance, including his future company secretary, David – would have been to sell the old place. 'And he did. Eventually,' David would recall. 'But it took years.' And as the birth of the car museum had demonstrated, he was equally wedded to his automobiles. There was only one notable exception – his beloved little Elva Courier racer, which he had reluctantly needed to part with before the move to Aden. Otherwise, what he bought, he almost always kept. He'd purchased the old, stone house and the barn in West Camel for a few thousand pounds. By the end of John's life, it was worth more than a million. But it was still in his and Annette's names, rented out to a succession of different tenants.

Another of the Haynes's Rules of Business was, on the surface, more orthodox. It was what economists call vertical integration: where a company owns all of its key elements of production and distribution. It was a hallmark of the early years of the automobile industry, under titans like Henry Ford. And William Morris. But John was particularly wedded to the idea. In part, it was a lesson learned from Haynes Publishing's first fragile months as a publicly listed company, when the print union strike had cost him tens of thousands of books. But it was not just a matter of business judgement. It seemed to reflect a deeply rooted drive to retain control. It was visceral. As a child, he had not been aware of all the setbacks Vi or Harold had had to overcome in their lives, but he had seen, sensed and lived with the effects, and that could hardly have failed to leave an impact.

The final principle that John applied was a focus on the vision he had for his company. That focus was unerring, and so was the vision. He would be the purveyor of his unique motor manuals; but also, through the acquisitions he made of other companies along the way, a leading *book publisher* as well. He wanted the Haynes name not just in car boots or garages, but on bookshelves and coffee tables.

At the start of the 1990s, there seemed no reason to doubt, or divert from, any of this. Business for Haynes was buoyant, on both sides of the Atlantic. His share of the US market was rising, and by 1990 it would account for one-third of the company's revenue. In Britain, the Thatcher government's supply-side economic reforms had cut income tax, kept interest rates low, and fuelled a boom in the housing market and in all shapes of consumer spending – cars included. Not unreasonably, Haynes was eyeing further expansion in America. For the first time, in 1990, he began moves to print on a larger scale in the US. At home, they'd been expanding as well, updating the printing operation at Sparkford.

All of this had meant, however reluctantly, increased borrowing, to the tune of nearly £2 million. And in late August 1990, John made the latest of his publishing acquisitions: a firm called Patrick Stephens Ltd. There was some connection, if fairly tenuous, with automobiles. One had particular resonance for John. Its co-founder, Stephens, had actually written a well-received book on how to build and race an Austin Seven Special. It also published motoring and motorcycling titles. But as with a number of his early purchases, most of its other books were about other things entirely: aviation, shipping, railways and military history.

That, in itself, need not have been a problem; it was undeniably in keeping with John's broader vision of the company as a book publisher. Once fully integrated, its titles might even contribute to the bottom line – although the evidence from most of the other acquisitions was not especially encouraging in that regard. The 'books division' was at this point losing about a million pounds a year. Still, Haynes Publishing, as a whole, was making money, several million pounds in annual profits. And its engine – the Haynes Manuals – was still going strong.

The problem was that the purchase of Patrick Stephens could hardly have been more ill-timed, for the engine of the British economy was about to stall.

The signs of trouble had been building, not least the fact that the dizzying rise in consumer spending had been funded by a steep rise in borrowing, and accompanied by steadily rising inflation. By the time Haynes bought Patrick Stephens, the spending spree had begun to flag. By the mid-1990s, the monthly sales of Haynes's book titles had fallen to their lowest level since the mid-1980s. In October, Britain moved to steady things by joining the European Exchange Rate Mechanism – a precursor of the single European currency that aimed to limit swings in the exchange rates among European countries' individual currencies. For the government, the attraction was that, with the ballast of a strong continental currency like Germany's Deutschmark, Britain's ERM membership might help bring domestic inflation back under control. But in order to keep within the agreed currency-exchange limits, in other words to maintain the value of the pound, interest rates now had to be kept at historically high levels, well above 10%. As the economy continued to slow, this left millions of consumers and homeowners, and thousands of businesses, unable to pay what they owed to the banks.

By early 1991, even sales of the Haynes Manuals were declining. As for the books, with dozens of releases now scheduled each year, they were in freefall. Stephens's other co-founder, named Darryl Reach, had been brought in to run all of Haynes's books division, and he now had to cancel more than a hundred new titles. But even more drastic action was going to be needed, and it would prove painful not just for the company, but for the man who had created it.

To say that John regarded those who worked for him as family is not, in his case, some PR cliché. Though he now employed many hundreds of people, a good number of them had been with him from, or very nearly from, the start. Given the depth of the recession, and the fact it had hit just as the company was further investing and expanding, there was no way around making major cutbacks, both in publications and personnel. As chairman, John would have to sign off on all of them, of course. But driving through a retrenchment of that scale was going to require key character traits that he signally lacked: an unalloyed steeliness and even, at times, ruthlessness. Those around him knew this. So, in the end, did he.

The man he tasked with seeing the process through was Max Pearce. A key figure in driving forward the US operation, he was also a veteran of the motor-trade business, having been a director of Halfords and having founded Haynes's main cash-and-carry customer, the Maccess chain. He had joined the

Haynes board as a non-executive director in the mid-1980s and had become deputy chairman not long afterwards. Now, he was given the CEO half of John's role.

No part of the company was spared his cost-cutting campaign. Book publishing was frozen altogether for a couple of months in early 1991, then resumed at a mere three or four titles a month. Commissioning was cut back and tens of thousands of unsold titles were remaindered. The Leeds warehouse was closed. Nearly a quarter of the workforce, including several senior figures who had been with Haynes since the beginning, were made redundant. Shareholders, too, were asked to pitch in. They were invited to take up a total of 100,000 newly issued additional shares in lieu of a cash dividend and, to John's and the other directors' relief, they enthusiastically did so.

Even some of the slower-selling Haynes car manuals were dropped. In order to further save money, now that the US manuals were being produced by a contract printer they'd engaged in California, the printing for most of the UK ones was moved to America as well. Still, it was a close-run race. Early in the year, an annual deficit of something like £6 million had been projected, factoring in the debt-servicing costs. In the company's end-of-year newsletter, John wrote that it had just endured 'the most difficult year in our 33-year history'. He was forthright in acknowledging that while the recession had had a major impact, this had been 'compounded and made worse by strategic decisions to expand the company into more general publishing'. That decision, he added in a triumph of understatement, 'did not work as planned'.

Still, by year's end, there was actually a pre-tax profit. It was not the £3.1 million of the year before. It totalled a meagre £26,000. But it was better than the alternative. In his newsletter summary, John confessed that there had been times during the year that he and Annette, Max Pearce and the other board members 'were seriously concerned that the UK company was on course to go down'.

*Chapter Thirteen*

# Turning Point

This corporate equivalent of a near-death experience was a turning point. This was not just because John Haynes would learn the lessons – or most of them – from how close he had come to losing the company that he'd spent decades creating; it was subtler than that. It was more of a refocusing, a recalibration of the compass, as he reminded himself about what he really valued, and wanted, for his future, his family's and that of his business.

The immediate crisis soon passed. Haynes Publishing not only survived, it began to post a series of record yearly profits, and John could take heart from the principal reason why: the move into America, which had begun with his and Annette's move to LA more than a decade and a half earlier. With the British market still sluggish, in 1992 US manual sales overtook UK ones for the first time. A year later, moving on from his contract-printing arrangements in America, and flanked by a smiling Governor McWherter, he opened Haynes's own cutting-edge printing plant in Nashville. By the mid-1990s, nearly *two-thirds* of the company's earnings would be coming from the United States.

All of that mattered to him. This was the same John Haynes who, from the day he sold his first Austin Seven pamphlet as a schoolboy, had begun jotting down every one of his sales in a little notebook. He was the John Haynes who *still* made his daily pilgrimages to his local Barclays to check the balance. But Haynes Publishing was more, much more, to him than a business. It was his business; it was a family business, his family's business. He never explicitly told any of his three sons that he expected them to make their own futures there, or at some stage to take up the baton; that was not in his character. Besides, the explanation he'd given Annette on enrolling J and Chris in Sutton Valence was genuine. He wanted them to be free, as he had been, to explore and to chart their own futures. And especially with all he'd learned about the complexities, financial and human, of steering an ever-larger business, he never contemplated simply parachuting any of his children into the upper reaches of management. He knew that wouldn't be good for the company. He knew that it wouldn't be good for them either.

But he did *hope* that one of more of them would ultimately ensure that Haynes Publishing remained *Haynes*; the boys could not fail to sense that. And beyond the closeness between the father and sons – the unalloyed joy that John, even in moments of personal or professional challenge, took from being around them – all three, in their different ways, did share his feelings for the business he'd established. J's first 'job' as a teenager was as a summer temp in the warehouse in LA. He'd gone on to apprentice in Nashville after university, and was now doing the same in the UK operation. He was about to leave – to join the corporate finance department of the tech-focused investment bank Beeson Gregory in London, then for a two-year MBA at London Business School, followed by a return to the bank as a director. But in John's mind, far from meaning his eldest son's path would *not* lead back to Sparkford, all of this would surely better equip him for a homecoming, if and when it came.

Chris's interests, and Marc's as well, were trending much more towards the expanding motor museum. While still at Sutton

Valence, in the late 1980s, Chris had spent his holidays helping to lay the concrete floor for the 'third hall' at the museum site. Having graduated when the 1991 business crisis was in full flow, and with a place secured on a leisure and amenity-management course at Loughborough College, he spent a gap-year working as a mechanic's apprentice in the museum. Marc, in the early 1990s, was at the midpoint of his business-degree course at Manchester University, and he was living a life that, even in a wheelchair, bore an uncanny resemblance to a twenty-something John Haynes. His university yearbook would list hobbies including 'boozing, sports and smiling'. A classmate, when asked to name Marc's 'perfect partner' on graduation, wrote: 'Becky... or that nurse (damn, forgot her name)'. But there was little doubt that Marc shared John's love for cars and, as it would turn out, for a museum that was jam-packed with them.

For John, too, the museum was about to take on a new importance. In the beginning, it had been more like a high-end garage, where he could finally bring together – and add to – his lovingly assembled variety of cars. And still savour driving, them, too. Mike Penn, who he'd brought in to run it, still remembers getting a memo from Haynes after just weeks on the job, saying that Haynes wanted him to ensure that all of the cars were in sufficiently good nick to be driven within an hour's notice. Having checked out all of them, Penn realised that, on a mere practical level, that was going to be a problem, at least if John wanted them driven safely. The cars ranged from the cherished AC Cobra, which was now part of the collection, and was 'all power and no safety', to the venerable Morris Oxford. That one, Penn noted, had 'a stopping distance of roughly 300 yards at 40 miles per hour'. Since he was due to attend his first trustees' meeting a few days later, he contemplated with some trepidation the prospect of having to tell his new boss no. When the meeting convened, however, he figured he'd at least give it a try. He told John that to make sure that all several dozen of the cars were instantly ready to drive simply wasn't going to be possible.

'Why?' John replied evenly.

Penn explained that a number of them weren't in perfect mechanical condition. Besides, there was the question of road safety.

'Well, how many can you get ready then?' Haynes asked.

Penn suggested he could manage six at any one time, adding that if any of the others were needed, he'd need more notice.

'OK, then,' John said.

Technically, for John to continue to drive the cars wasn't a problem. One of the advertised strengths of the museum, especially as it got bigger, was that the cars there weren't just exhibition pieces. They were fully functional, and even the oldest models were assiduously kept that way. Still, there were limits to which car John could reasonably use, when, and for how long. That was an adjustment for him. Even Chris and Marc, when they did go on to play major roles at the museum, would sometimes have to rein in their father's desire to take a particular car out for a spin. 'What do you *mean*?' Haynes would ask when they demurred. 'They're my cars!' At which point they would gently remind him that actually, no, they *weren't* his cars any longer; they belonged to the museum charity.

There was another adjustment required as well. Penn may not have known anything about running a museum when he got the job, but he was a quick study. Focusing on the curating and exhibiting side, he was determined to help John create as fine a motor museum as anywhere in the world. John's passion lay in what Margaret Thatcher's economic gurus might have called the 'supply side'. His principal focus – his joy – was in scouring every auction catalogue, spotting every car-sale advert, that might allow him to add yet another gem to the collection.

The acquisitions were eclectic, ranging from modern racers to classics from the dawn of the automobile age. Still there were a few cars that John especially coveted, in the same way that, before the museum, he'd so wanted to possess the AC Cobra. None, even the Cobra, had fascinated Haynes so much, for so long, as a particular American classic. Introduced with unfortunate timing on the eve of the Great Depression, the Duesenberg Model J was intended as a rival in its mix of power, elegance and elan to Britain's Rolls-Royce. And, depression or not, it did go on to become a status-symbol possession for figures ranging from Howard Hughes and Mae West to the newspaper tycoon William Randolph Hearst and the gangster Al Capone. But finding one of them for sale, particularly one of the early models, was exceedingly rare. When they did emerge, they were also very expensive. Though neither John nor he realistically expected to succeed, Penn was under standing orders to be on the lookout, just in case.

In early 1994, there was a small advert in *Classic Car* magazine. It was not only offering a 1931 Model J for private sale, the Model J in question was known as the Derham Bodied Tourster. Only eight of them were made, and this one had also been the first classic vehicle purchased by Otis Chandler. The Chandler family were the owners of the *Los Angeles Times*. Otis had been its celebrated, ground-breaking publisher for two decades. He'd retired in 1980 and had gone on to pursue a dizzying array of mostly sporting interests. Although he was then in his early fifties, he had even begun racing cars. He also resumed an earlier taste for collecting them, even opening a private museum of his own west of LA. He'd long since sold the Duesenberg, but regretting it, had bought another for his collection. His first Duesenberg was now in the hands of a wealthy east-coast businessman who had a car collection of his own, and Penn was dispatched to the States. He spent nearly a week going over every centimetre of the vehicle, even making sure that the manufacturer's unique 'J' numbers appeared on every one of its parts. Except for the tyres, the battery and the headlight glass, every bit was still from the original.

John was phoning every evening to check on his progress, clearly becoming more excited with each passing day at the prospect of finally finding the elusive Duesenberg. The final price tag – $500,000 – was steep. In fact, John had nothing like that amount of ready cash. Yet he arranged for a short-term loan from Singer & Friedlander for $300,000 of it, with Annette happily pledging her Haynes shares as security, and the deal was done. All that remained was to fly the car back to its new home. 'It is not,' John told Penn sternly, 'going to come by sea! And you are to fly back with it.' He did, and it turned out to be quite a flight. He strapped the car into the belly of an Air France Boeing 747 cargo jet along with its only other cargo: a group of thoroughbred racehorses held in check by a diminutive, but undeniably cheery groom. Still, the on-board food and wine were French, and very good. And the usually time-consuming ordeal of getting the car through customs at Heathrow lasted only moments. The officers took one whiff of Penn – unbathed for days, and now wreathed in the aroma of the horses – and waved him through.

The Duesenberg instantly claimed pride of place in the museum, challenged only by one earlier, decidedly less expensive, acquisition. This one as well, Mike Penn had been told should be on his watch list. It was not anywhere near as iconic as the Duesenberg. Still, it promised to be at least as difficult to track down. On this occasion, the target wasn't just a particular make or model of automobile. It was a particular vehicle: a little sports car that no one – or at least no one who John knew – had seen or heard of for more than twenty years. But it had played a special part in his life. It was the last car he'd raced: the Elva Courier that he'd had to sell before heading off to Aden in the mid-1960s.

At least Penn had one clue, if he ever got close; John remembered its registration number – 27 ALO.

Along with the ever-present stack of auction catalogues on his museum desk, Penn subscribed to a wide assortment of specialist motoring publications. He had become an especially avid reader of articles about the history of car racing. One early-December morning, he came across a small item about an old Elva Courier owned by a certain Mr Bird, a couple of hours north.

The next Saturday morning, without telling John so as not to get his hopes up, he made his way up the M5 motorway. His first sight of the car was hardly encouraging. It was at the back of a lock-up garage. The tyres were flat. The engine and running gear were a mess, and its fibreglass body looked like it'd been pelted by stones. But its registration plate was undamaged. And it read: 27 ALO.

Penn walked away, trying to hide his excitement so as not to jack up the price, and said he'd be back in touch within a day or so. After returning to the museum, he phoned Haynes at home to share the good news. But John was out, and Annette answered. 'Buy it, Mike,' she told him. 'And *don't* tell John. Just get it back, and get it fixed up. I want it to be a present.' The fixing-up part wasn't a problem. Mike had hired the first of what would become a team of gifted mechanics and restorers shortly after the museum opened. But they obviously couldn't do the work on the museum's premises, since John was always dropping in, visiting 'his' cars and generally monitoring progress, so the Elva was shuffled between Mike's house and a number of his friends' garages, until Annette's grand unveiling, on Christmas Day.

Yet despite the personal highlights – the recovery of Haynes Publishing; watching his adult children strike out into the world, with at least the good possibility that one or more of them might follow in his footsteps; and of course the acquisition of the Duesenberg – 1994 had had a bittersweet beginning.

Though John and his brother, David, had spent much of their youth separated from their parents, over the years they had grown closer to them. John's decision to send two of his own sons to Sutton Valence was at least in part a reflection of his own renewed closeness to his father, Harold. That relationship had become even more important to both of them since Vi's death nearly six years earlier. Harold was now in his late nineties, and increasingly frail, but still alert and engaged. He was especially pleased when John told him that he and Annette were intending to travel to Ceylon at the end of February 1994. John had last been there as a boy and hadn't been back since leaving for boarding school in England. Around the time he turned twenty, when he was at RAF Bruggen, he did plan a trip to see his parents and Mary there but, to the family's disappointment, he'd had to call it off at the last moment. Now, he and Annette would in a sense be making that right. When he'd told his father about the trip, Harold had smiled. There was a much younger man's glint in his eyes, and he regaled John and Annette with a store of old, tea-country anecdotes and a list of places they must absolutely go to see.

The afternoon before they were due to leave, however, David dropped in to see Harold at the little bungalow-style home in West Camel and found him more lethargic than usual. He immediately phoned John, who rushed over from Sparkford – only to see his ninety-eight-year-old father peacefully pass away. They promptly decided to cancel the trip to Ceylon, but as friends and neighbours heard the news of Harold's death, one of them, who lived just across the street, called Annette. 'Now, listen to me,' she said. 'I was talking to Harold a few days ago. And he said to me: I do hope that I don't do something silly to stop John and Annette from going to Ceylon.'

So they went, and made plans for a proper burial and memorial when they returned. The first few days in Ceylon were terrible, with both John and Annette feeling that – while knowing how important to Harold the trip had become – their place now was back home. 'We spent the first week more in tears than anything else,' Annette recalls. But there was another powerful emotion as well, a kind of reconnection with John's childhood and a sort of tribute to the father who had been its centrepiece. They hired a taxi and visited all the places he could remember from those early years: the tea plantations, the prep school, even the convent school where he'd learned to abhor both the nuns and bananas. And, the stately old hotel at Mount Lavinia. 'With all the sadness, it was actually still wonderful.'

And in a way, that could be said of John's life in general in the middle years of the 1990s. It is true that he had now lost both of his parents. But there was the consolation of having grown nearer to them as the years passed. And in some ways, he must have felt he was now enjoying the marathoner's equivalent of a second wind. He'd met, and got through, the 'wall' that seemed inevitably to loom in the final part of a long and gruelling run: in this case, not just his parents' passing but the near-collapse of the company.

The business was thriving again. The museum was growing, too. More importantly, John himself was growing not just in his enthusiasm for it, but his understanding of it as something much, much more than a grand garage. Having acquired the land around the original site, in the early years he'd kept adding new halls to accommodate the expanding collection of vehicles, but barely had new space been added than it would fill up with additional purchases. The rooms would get so tightly packed that museum volunteers could barely squeeze in between vehicles to make sure they were cleaned properly.

By now, however, things had changed dramatically. At first, it happened piecemeal. Given the claim that every one of the vehicles in the collection was drivable, not to mention John's personal interest in their roadworthiness, the museum obviously needed to find some additional help. The first recruit was a local barman who claimed, correctly as it turned out, to have apprenticed as a mechanic. Gradually others were added, until there was a fully fledged garage. Then, came a stroke of luck. A bypass was being built to bend the A303 trunk road around Sparkford, and a deal was struck with the construction team: they could park their heavy vehicles on still-unutilised scrubland behind the museum, in return for helping build a small test track when they left.

There were other add-ons as well. The first was a book store. John was initially not keen. He thought it would be out of place. This was a motor *museum*, and that should be its sole focus. Yet, in part because Annette weighed in, he changed his mind, persuaded by the idea that this would, after all, be just the latest incarnation of his venerable Motoring Bookshop. Finally, they added a small café. Dubbed the Pit Stop, it was an attraction not only for visitors but for a good number of locals, including an especially good number of local senior citizens with no discernible interest in the cars.

The transformation got a major boost, starting in the mid-1990s, with the arrival of two of John's sons, and the manner in which they arrived spoke volumes about John's feeling for, and his relationship, with each of them. Some wealthy parents indulge their children. Others choose 'tough love'. John had little time for either. As adults, he never coddled them, but that was not a conscious act of discipline.

Coddling was instead an instinct that he felt he had to resist, or at least most of the time. He wanted to give them the freedom, and the tools, to succeed on their own.

Marc was the first of the two to join the museum, in the summer of 1995, with an honours degree in business from Manchester University, shadowing Mike Penn before assuming a more formal role.

Chris's arrival a couple of years later was slightly different. The plan had been for Mike to take him, too, under his wing with a view to his going on to a senior role, especially since he was bringing clearly relevant skills from his leisure-industry course at Loughborough. But he began in the equivalent of the engine room: working alongside the team of mechanics in the workshop garage. Only then did he move on, with responsibility for the museum's development as a self-sustaining business. He helped expand its conference and hospitality programmes as well as setting up a range of special events including motoring tours for classic car enthusiasts. He also launched a museum newsletter entitled, with a nod to the new crown jewel of the collection, 'The Duesey'. All of this, he did in tandem with Marc, who became the museum's business manager and soon its overall CEO.

And as if this source of fatherly pride weren't cause enough for John to feel re-energised and reinvigorated, an impressive cream envelope had arrived through the letterbox at Coombe in the spring of 1995. Annette opened it. In the June Queen's Birthday Honours list, John Harold Haynes, Chairman, Haynes Publishing Group plc, was to receive an OBE: Officer of the Most Excellent Order of the British Empire.

'What's it for?' John asked her, genuinely bemused although also obviously pleased. 'Services to publishing,' she replied. Then, smiling, she added the old English quip about the OBE: 'for other buggers' efforts'. He laughed. Both of the replies, they knew, rang true. His company could never have survived and thrived without the help of those closest to him, and the many others around him whom he had inspired. Equally, without John, it would never have succeeded, or indeed existed, at all.

Yet, even as the profits rebounded and rose higher over the last few years of the century, a new crisis – a second marathoner's wall – would soon loom.

*Chapter Fourteen*

# COURSE CORRECTION

This time, the crisis grew in part from success.

For a quarter of a century, Haynes had been systematically expanding its reach in the American car-manual market – dominated, when John had made his first serious moves there, by a pair of powerful US competitors. He'd seen off the first of them, Clymer, at the end of the 1980s. It had given up car books and concentrated only on its still lucrative motorcycle manuals. Then, Haynes had turned its full attention to the long-time leader, Chilton.

John was always confident of the eventual outcome. His manuals – with their hands-on, dismantle-and-rebuild approach, all clearly illustrated and explained – had an appeal that no competitor could match. He'd backed that confidence, first with his editorial and warehousing headquarters in LA and even more effectively by providing for storage, distribution and finally printing in Nashville. By the second part of the 1990s, Haynes manuals had not only managed to match Chilton, they'd captured nearly two-thirds of the US market. And crucially for the financial health of the whole Haynes publishing group, the American operation was now accounting for the lion's share of the company's profits.

There remained one small problem, however: the war with Chilton was not quite won. With Haynes demonstrably pulling ahead of Chilton, there did seem a chance, briefly, that an amicable solution was within reach. Haynes offered to buy out its competitor, and Chilton, in principle, agreed. But both companies accepted that if the deal seemed likely to run into delays due to regulatory questions, they'd call it off.

That's what happened. Rather than surrender, Chilton, which had joined the enormous Disney corporate empire, proceeded to mount a fierce and final fightback. It began aggressively undercutting the Haynes manuals on price, to ensure that the key motoring retail chains didn't switch loyalties. Haynes fought back, of course. It secured important beachheads, picking up two of the major chains that had long been Chilton outlets. But that came at a cost, since Haynes, too, had to slash its prices to compete. The result was that in the final year of the 1990s, overall profits fell by 15% – because US profits, which had become central to the company's fortunes, had fallen off by nearly 20%.

If John, or the rest of the board back in Sparkford, were worried, they didn't show it. Indeed, whatever else they may have learned from their brush with bankruptcy a decade earlier, at least one lesson appeared to have gone unheeded. Back then, they'd turned things around by retreating from an aspect of the business that had always been especially important to John: the *non*-motor-manual business. His *book*-publishing. But despite the escalating battle with Chilton in the States, Haynes Publishing began the new century with its largest such acquisition yet. It paid more than £4 million to acquire a company called Sutton. Based in Gloucestershire, it was a well-established, well-respected publisher. It was releasing several hundred new books each year. It had a backlist of more than 2,000 titles. But they were not car manuals. In fact, they didn't focus on motoring at all. Sutton published works on history.

To be fair, there was a defensible business argument for the purchase, beyond John's undiminished desire to be a publisher of books that covered more than just engines and gearboxes. The logic for the future of his manuals business dictated that at some stage – in financial terms, the sooner the better – all of the manuals would be printed not in Sparkford, but at his more efficient, and more economical, plant in Tennessee.

Part of the reason John was attracted to buying Sutton was because, once it was integrated into the Haynes operation, Sparkford could be used to print *its* books, and the idea of simply having to close the Sparkford printing operation pained him. It was a part of his company's history. And there would be a human cost, too. Having had to let go of dozens of long-time, loyal employees during the emergency cost-cutting of the early 1990s, the last thing he wanted to do was to have to deliver the same message to the more than fifty printing staff just a few floors down from his office in Sparkford.

But there was soon an even larger hit to Haynes's balance sheet. This one, at least, involved an acquisition that was undeniably worth making. Early in 2001, for $14 million, John finally won the war of motor-manual supremacy in the United States: Haynes bought Chilton.

Still, the *short*-run was not looking good. In its accounts at the end of its financial year, in May 2001, Haynes reported a loss of £700,000 – the first annual loss in its history. And there was borrowing to worry about. Despite John's abhorrence of debt, the company had at times borrowed over the years. Yet it had never done so on the scale required to secure victory over Chilton in the States. It now owed more than £10 million to the banks. Worse, this came at a time when UK profits were *down* by roughly £1.5 million. One of the major motoring chains in Britain, Haynes's second-largest domestic customer, had gone bust, and that hadn't helped, but the main drag on revenues was Sutton.

And the main need was a coherent new *strategy*: a core definition of a company, which had grown, developed and expanded over the years, largely on the impetus of the instincts and intuition of one man.

The change, both for John's company and his family, was always going to happen at some stage. But especially given the expectation that US profits would now recover and accelerate – which they did – it did not necessarily have to come so soon. The problem was the uncertainty surrounding the original, UK business. That showed no immediate sign of getting back into profit, and John himself saw the need for a fundamental rethink.

The first, dramatic sign had come in a phone call which he made in September 2000 to a man he'd never met. Eddie Bell was one of the most prominent, and colourful, figures in British publishing. He had just turned fifty-one, but suddenly had time on his hands. He had parted ways a few months earlier with HarperCollins, which he'd run for the last decade. He was now in the process of planning to open a literary agency, and was having breakfast with his wife when the phone rang. 'Hello,' the voice on the line said, 'I'm John Haynes. We've never met. But I have a business that is very like HarperCollins. It's a lot smaller,' he added quickly, 'but very like HarperCollins, with all its intricacies. And it's become very complicated, so I'd like you, if you would, to come down and have a look, and join my board as a non-executive director.' It was, as Bell recalls, completely out of the blue. But a month or so later, he boarded the train to Sherborne, just a few miles down the road from Sparkford, where he was met by a driver 'in the oldest, and most beautiful, Rolls-Royce' Bell had ever seen.

That first full day that he spent in Sparkford provided striking insights into the business, but also into the man who'd created it. What most struck Bell was John's grasp of – and pride in – every aspect of the company. Impeccably dressed in a dark blazer and tie, Haynes greeted him with his trademark smile and led him upstairs into his office. It was, Bell recalls, something of a mix 'between a car mechanic's office and a publisher's'. It was also anchored, he couldn't help noticing, by a woman with a disarming smile and an obvious command of the multiple demands on Haynes's time and attention: his long-time personal assistant, Sandra MacKinnon.

Then he was taken on a grand tour, beginning with the printworks, at which point John turned and asked him: 'What do you think of it?'

'Can I be candid?' Bell replied.

Smiling again, John said, yes, of course. When Bell said that it was fine – 'a bit dated, but it still works' – Haynes nodded and proceeded to reel off precisely how many volumes it could handle per day, and how it could also provide high-quality colour printing. The walk-round took well over an hour, with John stopping frequently to speak to employees. 'That man's been here for more than twenty years,' he told Bell. 'And *this* one,' he said, motioning toward a trim, balding man named John Warry, 'he's been here for thirty years, from the beginning!' Warry had been hired three days before his sixteenth birthday, in the spring of 1970, as an apprentice in the printing operation, just as it was being moved from Lower Odcombe to the converted barn at Camway. He'd had a series of gradually more senior roles and had been promoted a year earlier to become overall site manager at Sparkford.

After a stop in the warehouse, they ended up in the books division, where the editorial staff was preparing the latest in its list of illustrated, coffee-table volumes on an array of non-motoring subjects. John turned to Bell and declared: 'We've just acquired a company called Sutton.'

For now, the future of Sutton wasn't an urgent issue, although that would change as Bell became an actively involved member of the board – first as a non-exec, later an executive, and ultimately executive chairman – in the years that followed.

At the first board meeting he attended, a week or so later, the issue was more straightforward: the move finally to purchase Chilton. The only question was the price, and when it turned out that the man in charge of Chilton had once worked at HarperCollins, John asked Bell whether he could give him a call and 'see if you can get a better deal'. Bell said he was sceptical, given that Chilton had probably settled on the asking price, but he made the call. It was as he'd expected. 'The price is the price, I'm afraid,' he told Haynes and other other board members, 'but it looks like there's a deal to be done and we should do it.' John's response would become familiar to Bell, on a whole range of management issues, over the years. He paused for a few moments and then said, 'OK. Great. Let's do it.'

The only thing that really bothered Haynes, even though he recognised it was necessary in this case, was the large loan they'd need to finance the deal. 'I don't like borrowing,' he said. And the flip side – again a familiar part of any board meeting where a major decision had to be taken – was a need for John to satisfy himself about the long-term health of the business. That concern had always been there, but became especially acute after Haynes's nerve-wrackingly close call in the early 1990s. Please, John would say, take me through the projected cash flow for the next twelve months. 'It was a constant with John,' Bell says. 'That, and the borrowing.'

But for Bell, there was also another, more striking constant, in the way Haynes ran the board meetings. It was, to put it mildly, a contrast to the high-powered meetings he'd become used to in his publishing career. 'He would put in his thoughts, and his opinions. But he'd just let the discussion run. He would *listen*. And he would never, ever, interrupt a debate, or argue with anybody.'

Chilton, however, was the easy decision. With far tougher calls still ahead, Haynes oversaw a further major reshuffle of his board at the start of 2002. Two key figures in the success story for Haynes in the US, Eric Oakley and Dan Benhardus, were brought in, as group CEO and group finance director. Another numbers man who'd joined in the 1990s, James Bunkum, was named finance director for the UK business. And the further change involved John's own family: his eldest son, J, became managing director for the UK.

There was another family transition as well, which was bittersweet for John. Annette and he had agreed, reluctantly, that she would step down from the board, especially difficult for both of them since she had been part of the business from the very beginning. But joining was another Haynes: Marc became a non-executive member.

Especially with J's new role, there was never any doubt that this remained *Haynes* Publishing Group. And John was still ultimately in charge, especially on the major decisions. But the reshuffle was a recognition that a new degree of rigour was needed to sort out the future of the UK business. And while he knew, deep down, that at least some of the necessary changes might be ones he wouldn't necessarily have made, J's presence provided both a sense of reassurance, and confidence.

Unlike the other two boys, J had never apprenticed at the motor museum. But back in the 1980s, shortly after it had opened, Mike Penn got a call from 'the boss' to say that he was sending along J, who'd just passed his driving test, to see him. John said he'd be grateful if Mike could help sort out a few mechanical issues with his car. He expected the teenager to pull up in Porsche, maybe even a Ferrari. Waiting outside, he could hear some other 'poor sod' labouring up the road with what, to Mike's ear, sounded like at least one end-bearing about to give out, only to watch a battered old Fiat draw to a stop in front of the museum, and the lanky frame of John Haynes's firstborn clamber out. Getting it in running order – replacing the 'big ends', without actually taking out the engine – was no easy task. But at John's insistence, and his son's transparent enthusiasm and determination, J did the job himself.

Fixing up the company's big ends took a good deal longer. It was made easier, at least, by the rebound in the States. The following year, the US operation made nearly £7 million in profits, affording the directors the time, and leeway, to chart its new course. In a portent of what was to come, one of their first moves was to jettison an offshoot of the company that had been formed only a couple of years before. The Garage Equipment Division sold Haynes-branded tools to motor garages. One of them, a fault-code reader, had won an industry 'Tool of the Year' honour, and sales were rising. At least in John's increasingly broad definition of the term, there was potential 'synergy' with garage-trade sales of the motor manuals. But there was an inescapable problem: the division was still losing money, and that showed no sign of changing. With both a business degree and banking experience, J also had a decidedly more restrained understanding of synergy than John. The garage equipment they were selling did carry the Haynes logo, but, as he pointed out to his father, that was pretty much as far as things went. They were paying for the software development, for instance, but didn't own the intellectual property. Crucially, they lacked sufficient experience and knowledge of the professional garage market to ramp up distribution. The logical move was to sell it off.

John, on his own, would almost certainly have held on to it, at least for a while. That was true of a number of other decisions – big and small – which J and the other three newly elevated board members, with Eddie Bell playing a steadily increasing role, would put to him over the next few years. But no single period in his company's life, not even the heady early years, more sharply illustrated the strength, and complexity, of his character. In a way, the first years of the business had been easier. Yes, money was tighter. Success wasn't yet assured. But he was still in his twenties. It was *his* company, or his and

Annette's. Focus wasn't an issue. They had one product, a kind of motor-manual they'd essentially invented, and the singular aim of producing and selling every last one they could. Now, he was the chairman of an incomparably larger and more varied business, with a financial responsibility not just to himself or his family, but to shareholders. He was also well into his sixties. He was surrounded by a new generation – among them, J, in his thirties – with different insights, different experiences, different ideas.

Sometimes, this involved little things, and relatively small decisions. One of the regular editorial meetings, at which proposed Haynes publications were either nodded through or nixed, Jeremy Yates-Round (the managing director) and several others, including Annette, championed an offbeat memoir, called *Flat Out, Flat Broke*. It was the story of a Cockney car enthusiast named Perry McCarthy who'd set out as a teenager to fulfil a dream: becoming a top-flight Formula One driver. In that, he'd fallen short. But McCarthy was a celebrity of sorts: he'd gone on to become the first 'Stig', the masked test-driver on BBC television's successful *Top Gear* programme. The book was a breathless – at time also hilarious – tale of trying and failing.

'Why on earth should we want to do a book on someone who *didn't* succeed?' John asked.

But in the end, he agreed. That mattered, and not only because McCarthy's book would become one of Haynes's all-time bestsellers; it was also because it went to the heart of what set John apart from so many other self-made successes. He was not alone in possessing the hunger, drive, vision and talent required to create and grow his business. But especially in these later years, he demonstrated a rarer gift: the ability to adapt. It did not come naturally. He was never one to step back, or stand aside. No less than before, he had his own instincts, ideas and strong opinions, which he was not shy in sharing. But as Eddie Bell had noted, he also had a talent for listening.

If presented with a reasonable argument, even one he'd rather not have heard, he would quietly ask 'why'. If the answer made sense, he would almost always acquiesce.

It obviously helped – in resolving the larger issues about the UK business's future – that the person on the other side of the table was often his eldest son, someone he loved, cared for, respected, and in whom he took great pride. But there was something else operating as well: the fact that he cared deeply for the *company* he'd founded, more deeply than he cared about running it exactly the same way as before.

Perhaps the main reason all this worked, however, was because the 'focus' of the changes he was being encouraged to make chimed fundamentally with what John sensed was right. Some of the steps taken were tough, none more so than the decision in 2007 to finally sell Sutton, which had yet to post a single annual profit. And J, who had become managing director not just for the UK but all European operations, also wound down Haynes's French-language operation, which was losing money, after nearly fifteen years. Some of the adjustment required was simply generational. Among the 'manual' titles now appearing were some that, it's safe to say, would not have occurred to John.

The first was down to serendipity: an approach by the Men's Health Forum for permission to use the Haynes logo and its manual style on a book, by a physician named Ian Banks, about men's health issues. The public relations agency they approached convinced them, instead, to partner with Haynes and make it a genuine Haynes manual. With its conversational tone and car-like Haynes illustrations, it was a major success. And a few months later, with J's wife expecting their first child, J came up with the idea of a follow-up: a baby manual, to equip fathers to dispense the same tender, loving care to their newborns as they'd learned – with the help of other Haynes publications – to shower on their cars. Also soon added to the Haynes list was a markedly different kind of HGV manual, dealing not with trucks but with strategies for portly men to shed weight. Then there was one that earned a front-page story in the famously laddish British tabloid daily, the *Sun*: the *Sex Manual*. John would surely not have embraced that idea in earlier years, but it was a reflection of the shift in the business's direction, and his own growing readiness to embrace it, that he celebrated its success, telling one reporter with a mischievous smile: 'It's like all Haynes manuals; only with this one, no workshop sessions.'

There were other new manuals. Some were tongue-in-cheek plays on the well-established, much loved, Haynes brand. One would become among the bestselling titles in the company's history: the traditional Haynes workshop treatment for a Royal Air Force classic, the Spitfire. Another, aimed at ageing would-be rockers, was on the iconic Fender Stratocaster guitar. There were spin-offs as well, like a £30 toy-and-manual kit aimed at helping parents and their kids build a true replica of an internal combustion engine. But all had something in common. Even though some of the new publications were in book format – and even though a toy kit was clearly a new departure – their roots lay in the product that had built John's company in the first place: the Haynes manual. That, John got entirely. And while it might represent a retreat from his desire to make the company a serious book publisher as well, it did fundamentally mesh with how he'd built the business. As the American country music faithful, down the road from his printing plant in Nashville, might have put it: *'You dance with the one that brung you.'*

Yet he recognised that one hugely significant change going on around him – the accelerating pace of technology, and especially the growth of the Internet – could very well make even that dance difficult. He didn't like it at all. Even when the business was in its infancy, when he was taking apart the cars himself, he'd draft in a friend to deal with anything electrical. His personal relationship with computers was always deeply uncomfortable, and usually at arm's-length. Email was becoming more widespread, but John wanted no part of it, leaving any such communication to his ever-present PA Sandra MacKinnon, the West Camel woman initially hired, in her teens, to help Annette with the company books. Even though bank account information was migrating online, he also still insisted on taking his daily, late-morning drive to his local bank branch, in Castle Cary, the tiny market down up the road from Sparkford. And while the march of technology was infiltrating car-making as well, with a more and more sophisticated use of sensors and computer management, John remained steadfast in his conviction that there would *always* be a market for his manuals. Even the newest cars would, after all, have to be serviced, cared for and repaired. More than this, he was sure that the *real* versions of the manuals – the ink-on-paper kind, the ones you kept on a garage workbench, turning the pages with oil-stained fingers – would survive. You could *hold* a book. Possess it. Cherish it. Keep it on your shelves. Try doing that, he'd say, with some digital imitation. As it happened, he was by no means alone at Haynes, or in his boardroom, in his conviction that paper and print would always find a home. And on that, they would turn out to be right, even with the embryonic rise of another tentacle of the Internet with obvious potential to compete: the video-clip pioneer, YouTube.

Still, J, who was further promoted in 2008 to group vice-chairman – effectively John's deputy – felt strongly that the company needed to make sure it could compete in the digital world as well. The key step involved another new acquisition, and an outlay of more than 6 million euros, then about £2.5 million. It involved a Dutch company. It was called Vivid – a name which, in a tribute to the wholesomeness of J's, and the Dutch entrepreneurs', upbringing, no one seemed to realise was shared with one of America's major porn-film production companies.

*This* Vivid was the perfect high-tech fit with Haynes. It was Europe's leading supplier of digitised technical information for garages on diagnosing, maintaining and repairing cars. Its enormous database was already being marketed in nearly twenty languages, and it had subsidiaries in Italy, Spain and Romania. John was predictably sceptical. Just as predictably, his response, once all the board discussions had been had, was: 'If you feel that this is the right thing to do, I agree.'

But there was another – and for John, a much tougher – decision to come. For some years now, all of the manuals were being printed, more economically, at the plant in Nashville. The Sparkford press had been limping along for a while by producing Sutton's books and taking in an assortment of job-printing orders. The idea of closing it, and cutting loose the people who worked there, was hard for John to swallow. Even though the printworks was now losing hundreds of thousands of pounds a year, he might well even have vetoed simply shutting it down. Even when a buyer was found, saving nearly all of the jobs, he did not hide his reluctance to sign off on the decision. But in the end, he accepted the logic, and agreed.

If John had a growing sense that the old Haynes Publishing – like the old publishing world – was fundamentally changing, he found the transition much less unsettling with his eldest son obviously poised at some stage to take over the helm. And one fixed point in his life remained unchanged, and the passion for it undimmed: John loved cars no less than when he'd first built his Austin Special as a Sutton Valence teenager. While the company he'd built around them was unrecognisably altered, he took renewed energy and enjoyment from his eclectic assortment of automobiles.

One new source of joy came from cars he couldn't even drive. They were made of wood, by a man named David Hayward, who had trained as a furniture maker but gradually built up a business creating models of automobiles. These weren't ordinary models, though part of the initial attraction for John was surely the echo of his own first, childhood foray into modelling, when he'd carved a Jaguar from a rudimentary kit on the tea plantation in Ceylon. Hayward's were works of art: accurate to the tiniest detail. John had first met him during a visit to the annual Goodwood Festival of Speed. Hayward had a few of his models on display, along with a sheaf of enquiry slips for potential new clients. John took to him immediately, and beginning in the mid-1990s, commissioned dozens of models of his most cherished automotive possessions: first, the AC Cobra, not long afterwards the Duesenberg; his old Elva Courier; and the car that, back at Sutton Valence, had planted the seed for Haynes Publishing, the Austin Seven Special. By now, many of the models were on display at the museum, but John kept a select few for the living room in Coombe.

But he still loved driving cars as well. Way back in the early 1980s, John and Annette had helped found, with a collection of close car-happy friends from miles around, something called the Southern Milestone Motoring Club. Until then, they'd all belonged to the Yeovil Car Club, which had been established shortly after the Second World War by a group of local businessmen who were automobile enthusiasts. Like other such groups, it organised excursions and events. But at least some of its august members were also – in John and Annette's eyes – insufferably full of themselves. The tension came to a head over one of their friends, a local garage-owner who had, among his several other cars, acquired a knock-off imitation of the AC Cobra. He'd spent a fair amount on fixing it up. It looked, and drove, wonderfully. But several of the prominent Yeovil Car Club members took umbrage, actually refusing to park their own *real* Rolls-Royces next to the AC pretender. That was the final straw. The response of the Hayneses and their friends wasn't exactly a guerrilla uprising, or the creation of some Popular Front for the Liberation of Car Enthusiasts; they simply walked away, and formed a car club of their own – the Southern Milestone Motoring Club – in which anything from a Mini to a Rolls, or for that matter a not-wholly-genuine Cobra, were entirely welcome, as long as they were cherished 'milestones' for their owners. The clue was in the name.

They started fairly modestly: with a four-day drive around North Wales, for which John and Annette called on the old 1930 Morris Oxford. It proved no better then than when John had bought it at auction in making its way up steep hills, at least in forward gear. But it was huge fun, and in the years that followed, especially once the major changes to his company got underway in the 2000s, they took dozens of other, longer excursions. Most were through their own car club. A few others through the RAC or various Jaguar-owner groups, in John's XK150. When it came to cars, especially once the museum was up and running, John was decidedly polygamous. But through all the many cars he owned and drove, the Jaguar, acquired just after they'd moved to Somerset, remained particularly close to his heart.

The geographic reach of their motoring tours was extraordinary. One of the first was a breathtaking late-spring road trip in the XK to Norway's Northern Cape. This one was organised by the Jaguar Club of Norway. Along with nearly a hundred other British Jaguar-owners, John and Annette crossed the channel, drove on into Germany and caught an overnight ferry to the Norwegian capital of Oslo, which was the starting point for the 650-mile drive up toward the Arctic Circle. The scenery – the lakes and mountains – was breathtaking. The spirit in the group was, mostly, collegial. But inevitably, as with any coming-together of certified car enthusiasts, there was a whiff of competitiveness as well.

In the early stages of the trip, on good paved roads, John had to accept that, while his XK150 was no slouch, it was also no match for the E-Types that routinely pulled ahead. Yet the nearer they got to the Cape, the northernmost drivable reach of the whole European continent, the brisker the weather, and the worse the roads became. Near the end, they were not really roads at all: only partly paved and strewn with rocks. It was, as Annette recalls, with undisguised glee that the XK150's higher ground clearance now gave *them* the edge of the E-Types. The final stretch to the cape itself – a thousand-foot, clifftop plateau overlooking the Barents Sea – had to be made by ferry. The air was cool, the wind brisk, but a few hours after their arrival, on the stroke of midnight, they were treated to the extraordinary spectacle of the sun still bathing the surface of the sea.

Another of their tours came in the summer of 2006, not long before the Haynes board began exploring the idea of acquiring the digital company Vivid. It was another of the trips that they took with a Jaguar club, and this one struck John and Annette as having the makings of a real adventure. Though the driving part turned out to be far tamer, and more limited, than their motor trek to the Arctic, it was a delightful mix of the beautiful and the bizarre. The destination was St Petersburg, formerly Leningrad: the north Russian city that got its old Tsarist name back after the collapse of the Soviet Union. They set off in late July from Stockholm, where Mike Penn had helpfully driven the XK150 from England to meet them. Then, they took the overnight ferry to the Finnish capital, Helsinki, in time for a briefing from the organisers on how they were to drive across the border into Russia the following morning. They were all instructed to fill up their tanks at the Finnish petrol station just near the frontier and then assemble at the lay-by just before the border. And once they crossed, *under no circumstances* was any of them to stop along the nearly 250-mile road to St Petersburg.

The Soviet Union might have gone, but it was clear that this was going to be a distinctly Soviet-style trip, regulated and regimented to avoid the slightest chance of any freelance exploration. From the moment they crossed, they were led by a Russian police escort. Surprisingly, it was not John, but another of the dozens of other Jaguar enthusiasts, who defied the edict and pulled into a Russian petrol station a few miles in. For hours, they were brought to a halt, as the tour organisers talked, pleaded, cajoled, and ultimately persuaded the Russian authorities that there would be no such future transgressions. Finally, the procession resumed. Again in perfect Soviet style, all the traffic lights appeared to have been set to green for their final procession from the edge of the city to their hotel: the old, splendid Grand on Nevsky Prospect.

The tour of St Petersburg and its surroundings – including the grand Peterhof Palace, commissioned by Tsar Peter the Great as a Russian riposte to the splendours of Versailles – went off smoothly. It wasn't a motoring tour: all the Jags were confined to a lock-up garage in the city for the duration. But it had its moments and, for John and Annette, its lasting memories. The night of their arrival, John suddenly had an urge for a Coca-Cola. He and Annette set off on foot to cross the road from the hotel in search of a shop he'd noticed earlier. They crossed through a dimly lit pedestrian underpass. When Annette, who was leading the way, turned to make sure John was still with her, she was startled to see two men converging stealthily on him from behind, 'John!' she shouted, at which point the pursuers turned and ran away. The Peterhof, however, was gorgeous, and the collection of art at the Hermitage was every bit as extraordinary as they'd expected. The roads on the drive out, to Tallinn in Estonia, rattled the undersides of their Jaguars. But at least no one tried their luck by trying to stop along the way.

Yet perhaps the most beautiful of all their car tours – in 2003, as the transformation of Haynes Publishing was gathering momentum – also proved unexpectedly precarious. It was to Austria. It began with a ferry from Dover and a drive across the continent to Salzburg, which was to serve as their base for an array of motoring excursions. On the first Sunday, the small army of Jaguars set off onto the twisting Alpine roads to the south of the city, which they'd follow all the way into Italy before doubling back later in the day. John's XK, typically, was among the first in the extraordinary procession. It was a wonderfully sunny spring day, and on the initial climb the car performed perfectly. At the top of a nearly 2,000-metre mountain, he and Annette pulled over for a few minutes to savour the view before heading downhill in the direction of Italy. The large Jaguar negotiated an initial series of hairpin bends serenely, before entering a rare section of straight road. A few hundred yards from another hairpin, John shifted down into third gear. Then he dabbed on the brakes. And again, more forcefully. Then, turning to Annette, he said: 'I've got no brakes!'

He shifted down again, into second, but they were still going far too quickly. The road hugged the side of the mountain, with rock face on one side and only a steep dive down on the other. John pushed harder on the brake pedal, but that did nothing. 'I've got to crash it,' he said, with remarkable calm. As the hairpin drew nearer, he veered the XK into a crag in the rockface, and it groaned to a halt. The whole right front of the car – *my* side, of course, Annette joked afterwards – was a wreck. The front wheel was scrunched in at an angle. It was Sunday, so the road was busy. Dozens of local motorists manoeuvred carefully by, gasping at the sight of the accident. As the other car-clubbers caught up, a couple of them managed to pull over on the straight section before the curve. With their help, and the local police's, they managed to arrange for a trailer to ferry the car back to Salzburg.

It was a close call. The next day, they found that two motorcyclists had gone over the edge on the same stretch of Alpine road later that day, and one of them had lost his life. But it was also a testament to John's remarkable record of good fortune when it came to motoring mishaps. There weren't all that many, but inevitably they turned out far less badly than they might have. The first, of course, was the Lotus crash at Goodwood, just before he and Annette got married. But it wasn't only the racing. As he began amassing cars for the museum, he and Annette developed something of a routine for the many auctions they attended. Annette and John would drive up together. Once he'd settled on a purchase, he always insisted on driving the new acquisition back home – that was part of the fun – with Annette following behind. After an auction near Oxford where he'd bought an especially cherished addition to the collection – the AC Frua, which was a later adaptation of his prized Cobra, on an elongated spring chassis – John predictably got behind the wheel of the bright-red convertible. Annette followed in a Bentley. They were purring along the M3 motorway. The road was busy. John was in the inside lane, and Annette could see him itching to pull out and pass a line of several lorries. So she pulled out to give him room. Suddenly, she saw the Frua's right front wheel come off and go spinning onto the main part of motorway. Somehow, he managed to steer it back inside, and on to the hard shoulder. 'Who knew,' he said once he'd regained his composure, 'that a Frua could drive on three wheels?' By then, he'd been reunited with the fourth. A driver behind them had slowed down, stopped, got out, grabbed the wheel, pushed it back onto the hard shoulder and simply driven on.

With some of the cars that he most coveted, and most mattered to him over the years, John developed something very close to a personal relationship. As with personal relationships, each had its own place, its own value, and at times its idiosyncrasies. The tie to the XK150 – recovered from Austria, and before long repaired and rehabilitated – was a lifetime commitment. He could no more envisage a time without the XK as he could imagine living without Annette. Others were a bit more complicated. Among all the makes on his eclectic automotive wish list, for instance, few held as powerful an allure as the Ferrari.

He had bought his first one, at Christies, back in the late 1980s. It was a seven-year-old 512 Berlinetta Boxer, and he joked at that time that one of the principal attractions was its number plate: 512 OAD, standing for 'old-age delinquent.' It was in John's favourite colour: red. Its design was dazzling: low-slung body; even lower-along cockpit; long, sleek front end, with pop-up headlamps. It was also powerful and fast. AJ Jeans, his mate from the hill-climb and speed races, remembers visiting him and Annette for a party at Camway just after he'd bought it. 'Come and have a look,' John gushed. He opened the door and swept a hand majestically outward, as if unveiling a precious work of art. 'A Berlinetta Boxer,' AJ said, 'that's a lovely car!' When John invited him to join him for a spin, AJ climbed in the passenger's side. However great its other attributes, the Boxer was *not* a triumph of practicality. John had evident difficulty backing it up and manoeuvring it out of the drive, since visibility through the narrow rear window was close to non-existent. Still, once they got out on the road, it shone. John drove onto the carriageway and set off towards Yeovil. 'He put his foot down,' AJ recalls, 'not over-hard, but within ten seconds, it was touching a hundred and thirty.'

Hell, AJ moaned. John replied quietly: 'I don't want to lose my licence. I'd better ease up a bit.'

But it was when they got back to Camway that another important limitation became clear – one that would very soon alter John's relationship with this particular Ferrari. John was a fairly large man, and had been getting gradually larger with age, and AJ couldn't help noticing that he'd found it a bit tricky to manoeuvre himself down and into the driving seat. But getting out proved even trickier. In the years that followed, he only rarely drove the Boxer. In the early 1990s, in the classic example of a win-win answer to a problem that obviously wasn't going to go away, he gave the car to his youngest son, Chris.

But there were other cars, and at least one other Ferrari, with which he developed a complicated personal relationship.

By the early 2000s, he had his eye on another, decidedly less cramped, Ferrari: a brand-new, bright-yellow 456 GT. In August of 2003, he and Annette arranged to collect it from the factory in Italy. It was a thing of beauty, and that was only part of its attraction. On the drive home, especially once they reached Germany, whose autobahns lacked the inconvenience of a speed limit, it was as if John was suddenly back on the weekend racing circuit. 'Let's see how quick it really is,' he grinned, as Annette gripped the sides of the passenger seat. The answer turned out to be 169mph.

John wasn't the only Haynes who fell in love with the new Ferrari. Annette was especially fond of it, and was soon especially delighted to be behind the wheel of the 456 GT, giving rides on the display track to guests attending an opening of a new exhibition hall at the museum. The sun was shining brightly on the museum's purpose-built track, and the assorted Hayneses, their friends and guests were in high spirits. It wasn't a real race. At least it wasn't supposed to be. But the presence of one particular Haynes – Marc, who was then driving a specially adapted Porsche 911T Race Car – almost ensured an element of competitiveness. The stories of what happened differed afterwards, and they have grown in drama and detail over the years. But as Annette tells it, 'Marc and I had a little coming together.' The damage to the canary-yellow Ferrari was not too drastic, and it was put right by the experts in the museum garage. Outwardly, John was unruffled. However, it was a bit as if a priceless painting had been damaged and, however expertly, restored: to an outsider's eye, the Ferrari didn't look, or drive, any differently to when they'd picked it up at the factory, but *John knew*.

And it clearly nagged at him. Before long, to Annette's regret, he parted ways with it. He swapped it for an almost identical model, in a considerably more sedate burgundy.

*Chapter Fifteen*

# THE FINAL STRAIGHT

It was a bit cool for early summer. A steady rain spattered on the windows of the breakfast alcove at Coombe. But by the time John and Annette, his board, and dozens of other long-time employees congregated in Sparkford that afternoon, the sun had broken through. It was 1 June 2010, and they were celebrating the fiftieth anniversary of Haynes Publishing. They were also marking another milestone: the man who had built the business, the man whose name it carried, was stepping aside as chairman, succeeded by his eldest son.

For John, it might have meant an ending. It's a fair bet that most of those who read the official announcement dismissed the bit about his remaining on the board as 'founder director' as little more than PR-speak, or perhaps a way of cushioning the blow. In fact, it was neither. It did mean that the executive decisions would now ultimately rest with J, but gradually, that had increasingly become the case over the past few years. It is true that the big ones – selling the history publisher Sutton, the printworks at Sparkford, or buying Vivid – had always been made in full consultation, and after intense discussion, with John. But none of that was going to change. And there would be further such calls to be made over the next several years, not least because of the continuing effects of the global financial crisis that had hit in 2008. Haynes Publishing had been weathering them much better than a lot of other businesses, and there were two main reasons they'd been so well set for the storm.

One was the Dutch digital company, Vivid – an acquisition that John had at first resisted but to which he had ultimately agreed, as both J and his partner, Eric Oakley, laid out the reasons for doing so in a succession of discussions over many weeks. The other was down to John himself: dominance of the large US market. So, too, was the core *idea* that was enabling the company to adapt to a changing environment: the Haynes Manual concept itself. He took pride in that, and also came to enjoy the increasingly imaginative, tongue-in-cheek spin-offs created by the editorial team – everything from a Haynes Manual on making a Christmas pie to a series called 'Haynes Explains' that included an 'Owners' Workshop Manual' designed for Brits to understand Americans. That one, amid a welter of workshop diagrams, included the timeless observation that the waist measurement of the Statue of Liberty was 35 feet: 'or, as Americans like to call it, medium'.

Still, the transformation of the business wasn't yet complete. A couple of years into the new decade, there was another key acquisition, one that John would undoubtedly have made himself. At a cost of nearly £6 million, they bought out the still-thriving motorcycle-manual business of the first of its old American rivals, Clymer. But there was also another major restructuring in the UK, one that caused John undisguised sadness. The general books division – the part of the business that he'd always seen as indispensable to its being a *real* publisher – was all but closed, with distribution of its existing list outsourced as well.

Even though his father was now retitled as 'founder director', it's not at all certain that J could have – or at least would have – gone ahead with that decision if John had explicitly said no. But even in his younger days, that wasn't who John Haynes was. He was indeed a man of strongly held views. He could be stubborn. Still, one of his strengths, and one of the reasons so few of those with whom he'd built the company had chosen to leave over the years, was a talent for considering others' views as well. He could also read a bottom line. He knew that, from that point of view, the coffee-table books that Haynes had been publishing – many of them having little or nothing to do with cars – were not pulling their weight.

Nonetheless, it was tough for him on a personal level. Though he did not feel he could object to the overall decision, he did stand firm on a few of the details. When he was given a list of the employees who would have to be let go, he spotted the name of one man who'd been with him for decades. 'Not him,' John said quietly: 'No.' And that was that.

Eddie Bell, who alongside J was becoming the most influential voice in John's ear, recalls how painful it was. 'John loved being a *publisher*, other than manuals. He loved publishing books. Our job, basically, was to point out that there was no profit in this. We needed to talk him through the reasons why we could not sustain this. And we knew we had to muster clear arguments. He took them on board. But you know, here we were, in a way slaughtering his baby. Still, I remember him saying to me, "If it's got to be done, in your opinion if this is the right way to move ahead, then I will fully support it." I knew it hurt him a lot. And it hurt him a lot to lose the *people*.'

That John continued to play an important role was not just down to his business intelligence or experience, though he had both, or even the fact that he was the 'founding' member of the board. It also owed to an asset that is more difficult to quantify: wisdom. The aftermath of the acquisition of Vivid provided an example. J and the others might not have known about the Dutch firm's porn-film namesake in the US when they bought it. But once that clicked, the obvious solution was to rebrand it as part of Haynes. When J asked his father, however, John counselled against moving in haste. 'Let's let them settle in, and see how *they* feel,' he said. He turned out to be right. At a board meeting a year later, one of the Vivid directors said that they'd decided they wanted to change the name. When J asked what they were thinking of, he said: 'Well, we believe we should leverage the Haynes brand, and still convey that it is a product for technicians and mechanics. We're thinking of HaynesPro.'

But shorn of his direct executive role, and freed of the day-to-day responsibilities that came with it, John's life did begin to change. For one thing, he had given up alcohol. This was by no means his first try, of course. But this time, it stuck. He didn't give up drinking altogether. In far greater quantities than he'd ever consumed in beer or Scotch, he developed a taste for Diet Coke: glass after glass of it, in which he'd audibly stir the ice cubes at board meetings. 'I suppose John had to be addicted to something,' Annette quipped. 'He never smoked. He certainly never took drugs. So he had his Diet Coke!'

He also had his office in Sparkford. He would invariably still leave for work each morning and return only at the end of the day, fitting in his ritual drive to the local bank. Yet even that excursion was not precisely as before. Finding himself using his beloved Jaguar XK, with its manual transmission, less and less, he'd bought an elegant Lexus SC430 (a V8 GT). It was by no means a racer – it had automatic transmission – but it could still get from zero to sixty in barely seven seconds. It was both comfortable and fun to drive, and it now became his automobile of choice.

Increasingly, his focus began to shift toward the museum, where he was soon overseeing a transformation barely less dramatic than Haynes Publishing's move from a small family business to its listing on the stock exchange. It became a labour of love, in part because his two other sons would play central, and perfectly complementary, roles in making it happen. Marc had been running the museum for more than a decade. Chris's first major position there, a few years later, was as business-development manager. While the charity that John had created provided the financial bedrock, the aim was to generate other revenue streams, like the garage and the café, that could be ploughed back into its upkeep and expansion. But for the past decade, Chris's focus had shifted to running another of John's business undertakings, an increasingly profitable foray into property and building called Haynes Developments Ltd. Now, around the museum project, his two sons' roles again converged.

Marc and Chris were quite different, each seeming to have inherited separate strains in John's own character, but he'd never hidden the pride he felt in both of them. From the time he was entering his teens, Chris did display a fondness, and talent, for one endeavour that his father definitely did *not* share: the good old English game of rugby. It helped that he was a big and solidly built child. Indeed, in one instance, having been selected to play for his county, he was actually kept off the field by the referee in an under-13 county match, for fear he'd physically damage their smaller, slighter opponents. But once he moved on to Sutton Valence, he was in his element. Though he was barely more engaged by the academics than his father had been, Chris not only played rugby there, he excelled at it. He became captain of the first team. For years afterward, John would introduce his youngest son by reciting Chris's school accomplishments. He had been a school prefect, head of his boarding house, '*And*,' John would add, 'you know, he was captain of the First Fifteen … Remarkable, since I couldn't even get into the thirds!'

The business quality Chris most shared with his father – the one that made him so well suited to the property and construction – was an energetic, at times almost feverish, urge to look for new possibilities and new projects. He'd taken Haynes Developments into everything from building and remodelling, and land acquisition and development, to project management, which was a natural fit for the ambitious expansion now being planned for the museum. In fact, he also ended up for a considerable period with an even broader role, because the remarkable life of his brother Marc was never immune to the medical complications that had been with him since childhood.

'Remarkable', when it came to Marc, is an understatement. A little boy who John and Annette had feared would not survive his teens was now in his forties. And if Chris had ended up with his father's restless energy, Marc had two other essential parts of John in him: an unflinching, joyous determination to overcome any and all obstacles; and an unshakable love for cars. Though he'd had to endure dozens of medical procedures large and small, he had not just learned to drive. He had become the first paraplegic to win an RAC racing licence. He'd gone on to race his adapted 911 on the Porsche Classic Championship circuit. Even after several accidents, he never contemplated hanging up his race helmet.

One of them occurred during testing at Pembrey Circuit in Wales along with Chris and J, whom he'd enticed to join him for several seasons. It landed him in hospital in nearby Llanelli. He wasn't seriously injured. But after X-raying Marc's back, the doctors were so worried by the intricate metal scaffolding they saw inside that, until his brothers explained his history of past medical procedures, they were reluctant to release him. Marc's response was typically pragmatic: in future races, he always took along a batch of his past X-rays so that, in case of further trouble, the hospital would at least know what it was dealing with. Even the demise of the Porsche Classic competition didn't deter him. He promptly switched cars, buying and adapting a bright-red Ferrari 360, and kept on racing, until he was advised by his doctors to stop. By now, they reminded him ever more forcefully, he had a complex lattice of metalwork around his spine and upper body: high-tension wires that could give out, and thicker metal rods that could snap and in effect rip his insides out. With this in mind, along with failing eye sight and a concern that his reactions and ability to compete were diminishing , he made the decision to stop.

Yet even then, he didn't give up racing altogether. He created from scratch, and then ran, a new British racing competition – the GT Cup Championship – for racing enthusiasts who shared Marc's passion to compete.

Alongside all this, he had managed to help fashion a motor museum that bore no resemblance to its earlier incarnation. In the early years, the change from what was essentially a convenient place to assemble all the cars and motorcycles had been piecemeal, organic. John had had the foresight to buy not just the former sawmill, but the old showroom space and the surrounding land. With the success of the museum's initial garage and workshop, in a lean-to shed out back, he decided to build up the structure in order to add another twenty yards or so of room for the cars. But he and the trustees decided on another use for the added space instead. They expanded the workshop operation, and designed it to resemble the old William Morris Garages. The initial plan was to kit out the mechanics in 1920s collarless shirts and moleskin trousers, but that idea risked falling foul of Britain's arcane health-and-safety regulations, so they settled on blue boiler suits instead.

As the museum evolved, John continued to provide the vision, energy and funding essential to its success. One of the further additions to the exhibition space drew on a quality which John had in spades: a finely tuned instinct for business and marketing. It was called the Red Room. 'You'll love it!' he told Penn. In fact, Penn recalls scratching his head, at a loss over how grouping all their sports cars by *colour* could be presented as part of the *interpretative story* the museum was meant to tell. But John's brainwave turned out to be spot on.

With the exception of the most glittering gems in the collection, like the Duesenberg, the Red Room would become the museum's most popular attraction. Shortly after it opened, his son J recalls accompanying him on one of his frequent walks through the museum exhibits, where he'd inevitably attract a stream of delighted visitors. When they got to the Red Room, John turned to the group that had congregated around him and, in an 'interpretative story' that even the most seasoned museum curator would have struggled to outdo, declared, 'You may wonder why there are so many red sports cars. It's because I wanted people to be able to appreciate their *form*, the aesthetics, the design – unencumbered by personal colour preferences.'

Afterwards, J told him that the presentation had been 'pure genius'.

'Do you think it was good?' John replied.

'Brilliant.' Then, pausing a beat, J added: 'But the truth is that you just love red sports cars.'

John nodded and laughed out loud.

Though the steady addition of new acquisitions meant that the museum could still not be described as roomy, by the early 2000s it had ample space to exhibit a good part of the collection at any given time. It was attracting tens of thousands of visitors each year. The bookshop and café were bringing in revenue as well, and the garage was doing ever better. Yet Marc was now about to embark on an ambitious expansion that John and his fellow trustees had been contemplating for nearly a decade. John had long since been persuaded to abandon the original facility's name, Sparkford Motor Museum. It became, first, the Haynes Sparkford Motor Museum, then the Haynes Motor Museum and finally the Haynes International Motor Museum. Now, they would create something truly worthy of the name.

Marc played a key role in moving the plan forward, which John viewed as essential to turning the facility into the kind

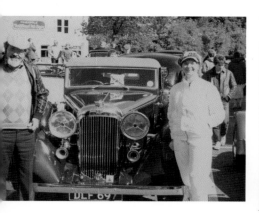

**Above** *On tour: Posing with Annette in front of their Lagonda LG45 on one of the first excursions organised by the club they co-founded with friends and fellow auto-mobile enthusiasts, the Southern Milestone Motor Club.*

**Right** *Driving rain: John and Annette in the Motor Museum's 1900 Clement Voiturette on the London-to-Brighton Veteran Car Run.*

**Below** *Northern delights: John with his treasured Jaguar XK150 during the motoring tour to Norway's Northern Cape in 1992.*

**Bottom** *Crossing in numbers: at the Estonian–Russian border during the 2006 Jaguar enthusiasts' tour to St. Petersburg.*

**Above** *Adjusting to celebrity: meeting Princess Diana at an event hosted by the relationship charity Relate in Taunton in 1993.*

**Left** *Going to bat: John and Annette at a charity cricket match in Sparkford with motor racing driver James Hunt and Haynes Publishing managing director Jim Scott.*

**Below** *Star turn: England cricket great Ian Botham flanked by Annette and Jane Marshall, whose Oxford Illustrated Press was one of Haynes's early publishing acquisitions and became a close family friend.*

**Above** *Flight plans: alongside Richard Branson at Los Angeles airport, in the early days of Virgin Atlantic, as John was putting in place the foundations for a major Haynes Publishing operation in the United States.*

**Right** *Getaway: with Annette on holiday in Marbella, Spain.*

**Below** *Museum milestones: with Tennessee Governor Ned McWherter unveiling the foundation stone for the new museum extension in 1988; (right) Annette, J and John with Marc when he opened the Veteran & Vintage Exhibition Hall; and (bottom right), with the motorsport commentator Murray Walker in the mid-1990s at the opening of a new museum entrance, restaurant and new exhibitions, including John's beloved 'Red Room'.*

**Above** *Family honour: at Buckingham Palace for John's OBE presentation in 1995.*

**Left** *Arriving in style: John's Bentley – with the appropriate number plate.*

**Below** *The Red Room.*

*Above Breaking barriers: Marc behind the wheel of his specially adapted Porsche racing car.*

*Right Racing legend: with Stirling Moss at the 1997 opening of the Motorsport Hall at the museum.*

*Below Vision fulfilled: the extensively redeveloped Haynes International Motor Museum, which opened in 2014.*

**Above** *Expanding the brand: John and Annette with Dr Ian Banks, who wrote the Man Manual, the first of a soon-growing series of titles using Haynes' trademark motor-manual approach to venture into other subjects, like men's health. Here, they're launching Banks's HGV, dealing not with heavy-goods vehicles but issues around diet and weight.*

**Left** *Milestone: with Annette and son J to mark the 50th anniversary of Haynes Publishing in 2010.*

**Below** *Racing colours: John and son Chris flanking Formula One driver Mark Webber at the opening of an exhibit at the motor museum of Webber's Red Bull racing car.*

*Above Birthday cheer: with Femke, the wife of son Chris, at a family celebration of her 40th birthday.*

*Above right Smart casual: not yet dressed for the occasion, John with Valencia, on the day of her wedding to son J.*

*Right Grandfathering: entertaining Augusta and Freya, daughters of son J, obviously sold on his insistence that there was a "dragon living in granddad's tummy".*

*Below Wide-eyed: welcoming his first grandson – Chris's son, Eddie.*

**Above** *Across the generations: John and Annette with their grandchildren (from left): Augusta, Freya, Nick, Chrissie and Eddie; and (below and right) the whole family at Femke's birthday celebration and a relaxed Sunday BBQ.*

of visitors' venue that would not only showcase its remarkable collection but ultimately make it financially self-sufficient. He, himself, had begun setting aside his personal company dividends to fund the nearly £5 million project. Chris's part, at first, was to coordinate and manage the redevelopment when, in 2012, the work finally got under way. But on three separate occasions – in 2010, 2011 and again in 2013 – he became the acting CEO. Marc had to go back into hospital for extended periods, and then increasingly needed to rest and rehabilitate afterwards in the pleasant, beige-fronted home where he'd long lived, just down the road in Sherborne.

The upgrade did cause dislocations. Some were inevitable, given the scale of the work, such as the opening of a temporary visitors' entrance at the rear of the original complex. Others were down to acts of God: flooding and near gale-force winds in Somerset. But by the time it was ready for its grand opening on a beautiful mid-April day in 2014, the metamorphosis was extraordinary. There was a largely glass façade – sleek and sinuous – in the shape of a car, as well as a new lobby, reception and ticket hall, flanked by the twenty-first-century incarnation of the motorists bookshop, with nearly the whole stable of Haynes manuals as well as Haynes-branded toys, gifts and souvenirs. On the other side of the entryway was the food and drink area. Though it was a restaurant in everything but name, it was dubbed Café 750, in a nod to John's long-ago guide to the Austin 750 Special.

The museum itself had also changed. Three entirely new exhibition areas had been added, and the collection – which had grown from John's initial twenty-nine cars and one motorcycle to more than 400 vehicles – was organised in themed halls. There was an 'American Room', another charting the 'Dawn of Motoring'; then a look back at 'Veteran, Vintage and Pre-War Classics'. There was an exhibit called 'Memory Lane' that brought together British-made family cars of years past; a separate motorcycle collection that included the world's largest single exhibit of Speedway motorbikes. And none was more visually striking – and none better captured the focus of John's automotive attractions – than the Red Room, with its visually arresting collection of classic sports cars.

And that was just the packaging. John and his sons' central aim was to make the redesigned and expanded museum more alluring to visitors, not just from all countries but of all ages. As part of its charitable remit, it had always run an apprenticeship scheme, whether for mechanics, classic-car enthusiasts or would-be museum employees, but these were now expanded. On the grounds of the new complex there was also a new children's play zone – Haynes Motorland – where kids could clamber in and over an assortment of vehicles, including the kind of JCB that had once lured a toddling J out of Camway and very nearly onto the nearby trunk road.

At the formal opening, the then-Minister for Culture, Communications and Creative Industries, Ed Vaizey, cut the ribbon and unveiled a commemorative plaque. But the real stars of the show were Marc and Chris, both beaming broadly; and, of course, John, who, in his remarks to the guests, was typically still focused on the future. 'Now that space is no longer an issue,' he said, 'I'm looking forward to continuing to build the collection.'

The redevelopment had also added modern office space. And while John continued to spend part of each day at Haynes Publishing – and remained an active voice at board meetings as *that* transformation continued – he began to spend more time at the museum.

In past years, he and Annette had often met for lunch at one of their favourite pubs. But now, John's midday eatery of choice became Café 750. There, and in his daily walks through the museum halls, it was as if the two major strands in his working life had finally come together. This was now the age of YouTube, the age of the iPad and the Kindle. But his hunch, his *hope*, was at least so far being borne out: people would always, he said, want the feel of an oil-stained Haynes manual between their fingers. Not just at the museum bookshop, but in retail outlets across Britain, the US and dozens of other countries, manual sales remained brisk. And if the Haynes business was now branching out, with greater focus on digital products through HaynesPro, even that was rooted in the original core concept of his business: providing unparalleled practical information on what made every car tick, and what to do when it stopped ticking.

What most touched John was the way that he, and his manuals, had obviously touched the now nearly 200 million people who had bought them. Time and again – at the restaurant, in the exhibition halls, in the entrance lobby – visitors who recognised him would come up and volunteer stories of how Haynes manuals had enriched their lives, or, in many cases, allowed them to buy and own a car at a time when they knew they could not realistically afford a big garage bill if things went wrong. And that, many of the visitors told him, wasn't the main thing. They would tell him about the special feeling of *involvement* which the step-by-step tinkering and repairing had given them, and the sense of accomplishment they'd felt when, just as the manual said, it all actually *worked*.

The museum provided a different kind of satisfaction. In his brother David's view, its final flourishing was no less important an accomplishment to him than the market flotation of the company. 'Although it was very much a hobby to start with, once it had the potential to be freestanding, I think it became more important to him.' Especially now that it had come to full fruition, it also tapped into a sense – like William Morris, in a way – that he was *giving something back*. He had begun the project with the mindset of the car-collector – something, as his remarks at the reopening made clear, which he very much remained.

But what increasingly animated him was the pleasure he drew from having gifted the cars he had loved and assembled to the museum charity. Or, as Chris often heard him put it, 'to the nation'. They would be there even when he was gone. Future generations of car-lovers, and their kids, would be able to enjoy not just hundreds of extraordinary cars; through the exhibits, and the educational and other programmes the museum was running, they would understand, and feel, the whole rich history of the automobile. And while it was not in John's character to say so out loud, it was evident to his family, and those closest to him, that John took particular pride in the fact that the Haynes name was on the entrance.

The museum soon entered a period of transition as well, however. Marc was there for the grand rededication of the complex in which he had played such a key role. But from late 2014, he was increasingly unwell. With Chris as acting CEO, he and John agreed that they should put in place a new team to take the museum onto its next stage. Marc remained engaged, if from a distance. Mentally, he was still well, but physically, he was weakening. 'He had this incredible, stubborn determination,' Chris recalls. 'Never giving up. He told me that, on quite a few occasions in his life, he could quite easily have slipped over to the other side – because of all the procedures, all the things he'd been confronted by. He felt he'd had plenty of opportunities, as he called it, to "transition". Basically, to die. But every time he was presented with that, he said: "No. Not ready yet." He'd accomplished remarkable things. He enjoyed his life. A lot. He would get very upset with people who talked about euthanasia, or that sort of the thing. He believed that if you were disabled, it didn't stop you from having a full life … And he *proved* that.'

What now most upset him – at times, terrified him – was that he began to lose his eyesight. Marc remained not only the titular CEO of the museum; he was on the Haynes Publishing board of directors as well. J began to go round to see Marc after each meeting and due to his failing sight, read him the minutes. But over the spring and summer of 2016, Marc's interest, and his strength and concentration, were flagging. In the autumn, it almost seemed as if he recognised that, after an extraordinary forty-seven years, his race was almost run.

He had said for some time that, when the time did come, he did not want to go into hospital. He'd seen more than enough of those. He wanted to remain in his little home on the handsome lane leading from the railway station to the shops and pubs and eateries in Sherborne. And on 16 October, he passed away in his sleep.

John, though so often reluctant to show, or sometimes even share, feelings of pain or sadness, was clearly deeply affected by Marc's death. Still, for him, as for the rest of the family, the weeks that followed were not only a time of loss and grief. Marc had been in so many ways a miracle. He had not only survived, for nearly five decades, against almost ridiculously steep odds, but he had lived more fully, and more joyously, attempted and accomplished more, than countless able-bodied contemporaries. With Marc, the funeral-parlour cliché – a death to be mourned, but also a life to be celebrated – actually held true.

The celebration was held a couple of months later just down the road at Sherborne Abbey – originally, a Saxon cathedral, dating from the eighth century. Both J and Chris delivered tributes, but the service concluded with an old Gaelic prayer, which John and Annette read out together:

May the road rise up to meet you.

May the wind be always at your back. And the sun warm upon your face.

The rain fall softly on your field, and, until we meet again, May God hold you in the hollow of His hand.

*Chapter Sixteen*

# THE OTHER SIDE

John's race was not yet run. Though he was now in his late seventies, there was not the slightest sign that, in Marc's words, he was ready to 'slip to the other side'. Yes, the sometimes breakneck speed of the earlier years had slackened. He no longer hankered to get behind the wheel of an E-Type, a Lotus or a Ferrari. Even his Jaguar XK. The pretty, and when necessary pacy, Lexus suited him just fine. Yet he was still a daily presence at Haynes Publishing, and an active one as 'founder director' on its board. While he was no longer the day-to-day decision-maker, he was still relied on for his insight, experience, his wisdom; and perhaps most often, for his combination of caring and calm.

He'd still regularly ask J into his office. 'He'd want to talk about something that he'd seen or read, or heard from talking to someone else in the company.' Yet he saw his role as no longer running things, but advising. As the business was navigating – with signal success – the aftermath of the world economic crisis of 2008, J went in to see his father to run through the list of belt-tightening actions he'd put in train. Agreeing that the necessary steps had been taken, John said: 'You just have to ride it out. And keep doing what we do.'

He was, 'pragmatic', J recalls. 'We'd taken costs out, and we needed to just keep delivering the product that people wanted.

And – as always – he said to make sure we "managed the cash" carefully.' All that was good to hear, but what J most valued, what he'd most needed, was the core message. 'It was calming …Don't panic.'

Chris, too, in running the property business, had similar encounters. 'You could go to him with your hair on fire, and inevitably, you'd speak to Dad and he would talk you down. Very calmly. Very quietly. Smiling.'

And it was not just his sons. Other long-time executives, or employees, would sometimes be called in. Even if John had questions ready for them – even if the questions implied criticism – the experience was almost always salutary. As one member of the museum team told Chris, 'You know, it's strange. When you go see him, you always leave feeling a couple of inches taller.'

But perhaps Eddie Bell put it best. In 2016, a few months before Marc's death, there had been a further board reshuffle. The HarperCollins veteran had got to know John well in the decade and a half since the sudden phone call that had led him to joining the board. He now became chairman of Haynes Publishing, with J as CEO. In Bell's view, John was 'an entrepreneur with a heart'. And he'd known and worked with more than few who had the first quality without the second.

John basked in the success of the museum as well. Its relaunch had boosted visitor numbers, but the expanded complex also made it even more attractive for the kind of corporate, or family, events – from company conferences to weddings – that Chris had worked to make part of its appeal. There were regular go-kart days on the test track. And its healthily beating heart remained the vehicles themselves, with no exhibition more successful than John's spruced-up Red Room.

But what drove him most, invigorated him, was family. The word was, for John, elastic. It embraced not only his blood relatives, but a host of friends, as well as members of the Haynes Publishing and the museum 'family' whom he and Annette had now known for years. Dozens came when, a couple of months after Marc's passing, they had a memorial service at Sherborne Abbey followed by a wake at the museum. Among them was Jane Marshall and her husband. Jane had owned and run Oxford Illustrated Press, one of the first book publishers John had bought, at the beginning of the 1980s. He hired her to help integrate it, and keep running it, under the Haynes umbrella. 'He was capable of saying no to one of your ideas,' she recalls. 'But he was great fun. Hugely supportive. And when you got his support, and his enthusiasm, it felt massive.' The Oxford Illustrated operation, along with the rest of the book division, was now gone. But she and John had not only remained in touch; in a real sense, she felt part of the family. A number of Marc's hospital stays in the final years of his life were in Oxford, where Jane now lived. She would visit him without fail, at least several times each week. 'The thing I most value about the years I was working with John was his *kindness*,' she recalled. 'You don't become successful in business without sometimes having to be ruthless, but he was immensely kind.' She wasn't married when she arrived in Sparkford, and on an occasion when a relationship ran into difficulty, she wanted to change her surroundings, and move house. 'But he called me in and said: look, let me loan you the money, and you can pay me back.' The finances were all done by the book. When it came to money, John was a stickler for detail.

Another woman, a few miles along winding roads and village lanes from Coombe, had played a role in one of John's regular weekly events. Her name was Mary Ashby. She was the landlady a picture-pretty pub called the Rose & Crown – a stone-fronted, seventeenth-century gem in Bradford Abbas. Nearly every Sunday, John and Annette would lunch there. Not only would Mary be ready with ample quantities of his favourite tipple – his Diet Coke – she had quickly learned not just his dietary preferences but his dietary main *weakness* as well: the one implanted in him seven decades earlier when Vi would whip up a batch of her home-made variety on the tea plantation. Shortly after they'd started going to the Rose & Crown, Mary created a bespoke masterpiece, never appearing on the pub menu, just for John. It included three flavours of ice cream – vanilla, chocolate and strawberry – covered with a veritable blanket of whipped cream. Sticking out on the top, in an uncanny resemblance to London's Millennium Dome, was an upright array of log-shaped biscuits, with chocolate in the middle of them as well.

On Saturdays, they would drive into Yeovil, where Jon and Sarah Palmer ran the elegant Pen Mill pub and restaurant, where John would always have chilli-con-carne, followed by ice cream of course.

But the core of John's family remained the children. You can chart the unbroken connection in the pages of the Haynes family's photo albums: John, then beardless and in his prescription sunglasses, cradling a one-year-old Marc, beside little J and Annette, in the south of Spain; a trip to Disneyland during a reunion in LA; a multiplicity of birthday parties in Camway and Coombe; Christmas parties too, including one with both John and Annette in full circus-clown regalia; Marc's university graduation. And, in these later years, alongside his five growing grandchildren, J's two daughters and Chris's daughter and two sons. John, without fail, is not just smiling for the camera, he's beaming. In fact, only an old Yiddish word comes close to describing the look: *kvelling*. It's an amalgam of joy and love and parental pride.

There are also pictures that tell of another, perhaps more unexpected, connection: send-offs when first J, and later Chris, left home for *his* old Kent boarding school, Sutton Valence. Annette had been understandably surprised at the decision to enrol them there. To the extent John had spoken at all over the years about his boarding-school days, it had not been with any great nostalgia. John's explanation – that it had given him the freedom to explore, experiment and find his own success – was no doubt true as far as it went. But there were other reasons as well. It would be an establishment of a kind of family tradition, a generational chain, something that had become more important to him once the whole clan – Harold and Vi, and his own children and grandchildren – were in the kind of close proximity that he and David had missed during many of their own childhood years. In a way, he may have seen it as a kind of validation, or a belated thank-you, to his own parents for the sacrifices they'd made for his Sutton Valence education.

He proudly followed both sons' progress there: the fact that they'd ended up in the same residential house as he had; J's march into the First XV in rugby, and Chris's achievement in not only making the first team but captaining it. At the end of 1979, he and Annette and the core team at Haynes boarded the train up to London for the culmination of their efforts to list the company on the stock exchange. Those around him were understandably tense. None of them yet knew what the response would be to the share offer they'd made formally a few days earlier.

John was sitting with Annette, and across from Murray Corfield, who'd worked with John on the day-to-day running of the company since very early on. 'It was amazing,' Corfield recalls. 'The rest of us might have had nerves, but all of a sudden, John opened his briefcase, the Gladstone leather case his father had given him. He took out a piece of writing paper with the Camway House letterhead on top, and a lovely fountain pen. Then, he apologised: "I hope you don't mind, Murray. I'm just going to jot a note to JJ at school."'

From very early on, he always took special delight in the personal connection with his children that mere distance had often denied to his own parents. When Chris was at Hazelgrove House prep school near Sparkford, John would delight in collecting him. Chris and his friends would be milling around outside as a procession of their parents drove through the gates and down the road leading into the school. Most of the parents were arriving in roomy family saloon cars. 'But if there was a red sports car, I could be pretty sure it was Dad,' Chris recalled years later. 'And usually my guess was rewarded by his beaming smile and a jolly wave.' On one occasion, the colour wasn't a tip-off. John had chosen to make the drive in the yellow Jaguar E-Type, predictably attracting the attention of not just his youngest son but an assortment of school friends. There was a slight hitch. Once he'd pulled up, cut the engine and emerged with a smile, he found that the car refused to start. Fortunately, he found no shortage of student volunteers to push it and bump start it. 'We went back down the drive, and Dad gave a beep-beep and a wave as the engine caught, leaving behind us a gaggle of young boys vowing, one day, to own an E-Type of their own.'

Once the boys moved to Sutton Valence, there was also at least a dollop of personal pride – and maybe a touch of vindication – in reconnecting with his old school. Since Sutton Valence was *not* Eton, it had not made a habit of sending its sons onward to Oxford, Whitehall and Number 10 Downing Street. To be fair, it could lay claim to a number of distinguished Old Suttonians in other fields. Some fairly well-known artists and journalists, for instance. Sportsmen, too, including the former England cricket captain Mark Benson and Sydney Wooderson, a runner who, for a time in the late 1930s, held the world miler's record. There was a fairly well-known magician among the ranks, too, and one graduate who had changed his name and gone on to found a Buddhist monastery. Even, in Sir Reginald Champion, a man who had been the British Governor of Aden after the Second World War. But John Haynes's own accomplishments meant that he was by no means out of place in this company. In 2010, he featured as the main interview subject in the alumni newsletter, recounting colourfully his own school memories, professing himself 'ever grateful to the staff and masters for letting me pursue my interests' and noting that, 'as a result', two of his children had now followed him there. Especially as the motor museum expanded, he also got more actively involved with the wider school community, offering it as the venue for a series of annual reunions of Sutton Valence alumni and their families.

With the approach of his eighty-first birthday in the spring of 2019, he had settled in to a new, less hectic routine – still going into his Haynes Publishing office in the mornings, making his daily pilgrimage to the local bank. Then he'd go to the museum, where he'd check on the latest changes to the exhibits and chat with staff and visitors who had often come to the museum as a kind of pilgrimage of their own, the natural extension of a personal connection with the first Haynes Manual they'd purchased alongside their first car. Then John would lunch at the museum café and return to Coombe for a siesta.

For a couple of years or so, he'd had an assortment of niggling health problems. There was nothing too worrying, but he was still on daily medication for his diabetes. He also had elevated blood pressure, and in the autumn of 2018, a routine test turned up a small heart murmur. On a half-dozen occasions, he had also inexplicably seemed to lose his balance, and had fallen. Still, John happily brushed aside the by-now-familiar medical advice that altering other aspects of his diet might be a good idea. Diet Coke wasn't great for him, he was told, at least in the quantities he was consuming. Ice cream either. 'His stubbornness was so good in some ways,' Annette would recall, 'but not so much in others.'

In mid-October, he came down with a cough, which neither she nor John at first thought much about. But it persisted, despite the usual variety of homespun and over-the-counter remedies, and a few weeks before Christmas he was prescribed an antibiotic. When that showed no sign of working, his doctor switched him to a different antibiotic just before the New Year. Again, there was no indication it was having an effect. So later on in January, Annette phoned and suggested they arrange a chest X-ray. John had the X-ray, but despite her regular phone calls, the results for some reason still hadn't come through by the end of the month.

It had turned bitterly cold over the previous week, and Friday, the first of February, promised to be even colder, with temperatures hovering around zero. Still when Annette and John sat down to breakfast in the alcove in Coombe, she wasn't particularly worried. She figured she would make another call that morning to chase up the X-ray results. It was only later that she attached any significance to one thing that she didn't merely notice, but actually remarked upon: grasping his fork, John's fingers seemed awkwardly rigid, something she'd not seen before. 'He had lovely hands – the hands of a pianist – but he seemed not quite adept that morning for some reason.'

'Are you all right, John?' she asked him. To which he replied, 'I'm fine, Nettie.' To all other appearances, he did seem fine. They agreed they would meet around lunchtime at the museum. They were due to attend a remembrance service at a nearby church for a woman who had for a time worked as a librarian in the museum, and with whom they'd remained in close touch, and then to host a reception at the museum for her friends and family. After lunch, however, John said he was feeling a bit tired and that he felt he didn't really want to go to the service. Since Chris would also be going, Annette suggested that she drive the three of them to the church in her four-wheel-drive Audi, especially since the roads were now icing up. John could keep warm in the car, and then they'd go back to the museum for the reception. But he thought it best just to go back home, so she said, fine, and they set off for Coombe.

Annette pulled into the large parking area in front of the house, and took the space closest to the door. She cut the engine

and had started to get out when she heard – rather than saw
– what happened next. There was a thud, and a sharp cry. 'A
shout,' as Annette recalls. When she rushed around to the other
side of the car, she saw John had slipped and fallen. 'He was flat
on his back.' It wasn't the first time he'd lost his balance, so that
wasn't what worried her. 'But he was obviously in pain. He'd hit
the back of his head, and there was a gash. And bleeding.'

'Can you move your legs, John?' she asked him. 'Can you
move your arms?'

'Yes,' he moaned. 'I can. It's my back.'

It was bitterly cold, but with the help of the live-in couple
they'd hired a few years earlier, she managed to get him to his
feet, inside, and into one of the comfortable living-room chairs.
She immediately called the doctor's surgery. 'Since he was on
medications, I wanted to know what I could give him for the
pain.' But it was late on a very cold Friday afternoon, and they'd
all gone home. She checked that the bleeding had stopped,
but he was clearly still in pain, so she phoned the emergency
paramedics. 'I thought: they'll come out. They'll take his blood
pressure. They'll check him over.'

They showed up with reassuring speed. With back injuries,
they told her, best be careful. They moved him into their
ambulance and took him to the hospital in Yeovil. Annette
briefed them as they went: about the blood pressure, the heart
murmur, and also the nagging, stubborn cough that had defied
two antibiotics.

Once he was settled in hospital, Annette reminded them
again that he'd had a lingering infection. And they did do an
X-ray, but not of his chest. Their concern was his back, and
when they got the results they told her they were worried by
a crack they'd found at the base of one of his vertebrae. They
kept him on his back over the weekend – presumably, to relieve
the pressure – with an assurance that the specialist could have
a closer look at him on Monday morning.

When he did, and checked Friday's X-ray, he said he was confident John's back would be fine. The crack was from an old injury, very possibly from when he'd crashed his Lotus just days before their wedding, but his chest wasn't fine. The infection had badly worsened. Over the next few days, Annette and the doctors discussed the range of other antibiotics they might administer. But he seemed, little by little, to be getting weaker. And as she sat beside him – often with J and Chris, their wives, and the grandchildren – what they all noticed most wasn't his physical condition; it was that, for the first time they'd ever known, he appeared to have lost his stubbornness, his thirst for the challenge, his eagerness for the fight.

On Friday evening, one week after he'd slipped and fallen, John Harold Haynes quietly passed away.

*Chapter Seventeen*

# GRAZED KNUCKLES

The speed and suddenness of his final decline were only part of the shock. Yet even – indeed, perhaps, most of all – for those who had known him best and been closest to him, it wasn't simply his death that left them feeling as if they were in a freeze-frame, or suspended in mid-air, unsure of quite what to do; it was his *absence* – the John Haynes-sized hole which he had left behind. This big, bearlike man, with his beaming smile and Santa Claus beard, had for years been not just a constant presence in their lives. He had been the mass of energy around which everyone and everything often seemed to revolve.

Amid the mix of grief and celebration with which Annette, J, Chris and their families remembered him in the days ahead – at home, at the burial in the church in Bradford Abbas, the memorial service at the church in Queen Camel and the reception afterwards at the museum for the wider family of John's friends from the different stages of his life – they began to move on. They each had their own memories, and in the long tradition of airbrushing that comes with mourning, very few of them fully encompassed fully what John was. He could be stubborn, self-interested, self-absorbed – he might not have achieved his remarkable business successes otherwise – but what made him so compelling was that he was more than that.

He was also shy. He was thoughtful. He was caring. He was

kind. Of all the reminiscences his family shared in the days after his death, one, from Chris, was especially telling. He'd been shopping with his father one day in Sherborne. When they'd finished, they were walking back to the car when they spotted an obviously inebriated man pouring brandy onto the front seat. Since the car in question was one of John's favourites – his Jaguar E-Type – Chris was bracing for what might come next as he hurried his pace. But when they reached the car, John turned to the man and smiled. 'That's a terrible waste of brandy, don't you think?' he said. The drunk nodded, smiled and walked away.

John's absence was felt in the business as well, although not quite in the way outsiders may have assumed. He'd taken a step back from day-to-day management involvement, moving into his role as 'founder director' nearly a decade earlier. J had become CEO in 2016, alongside Eddie Bell as chairman, but both continued to consult frequently with John, drawing on his insights, his experience, his unparalleled ties to the business he'd founded, and on his support for seeking to map out its future.

The balance sheet was looking good. Over the previous few years, the world's single most respected brand in automotive care and repair had girded itself for the changed twenty-first-century market. Revenues, at £36 million in the previous year, and profits, at £3.6 million, were on the rise. It had nearly £5 million in the bank. Yet with the prospect of intensifying competition in the high-tech areas that were increasingly predominating, they faced an obvious challenge. Haynes, for all its accomplishments, lacked the size to compete head-on with the major players in this new technological universe.

During the months before John's death, J had begun discussing the idea with his father of selling the company – in effect ensuring the future of the Haynes brand in the hands of a corporate buyer with greater reach and much deeper pockets. John's heart must have told him no, but, as with so many of the tough choices the business had faced since he'd stepped down as chairman, his response was measured, thoughtful.

The key, he said, was what would best serve the business's interests: the future of the special place that Haynes manuals, whether in print or in digital form, occupied in the lives of millions who loved cars as much as he did; and the financial future of the employees who, for decades, had helped him build and expand the company. As long as the price was sufficient to deliver both of those goals, John told his son, then it was right to consider a sale. And they were considering it. Just a couple of days after John's fall, ahead of a regular Haynes board meeting, J and Eddie had been due to meet him and go over a document outlining the process for selling the company.

They did not move quickly. The absence of John, not just from the business but from the lives of all who worked there at every level, focused minds on simply carrying on, ensuring that the upward trajectory they'd charted continued smoothly. It was not until November 2019 – nine months after his death and not long before the sixtieth anniversary of the company he'd created, that Eddie Bell formally announced the decision to sell. 'The board believes our future will be best secured by the whole group becoming part of an organisation with the financial resources to invest for future expansion and take the company through to the next sixty years of success.'

In mid-February of 2020, Haynes Publishing announced a sale had been agreed. Valuing the company at £7 per share, a premium of more than 62% over its market level at the time, the price tag was nearly £115 million. The purchaser was one of Europe's top technology players in the automotive aftercare market, the French firm Infopro Digital.

But John's death was also felt much more widely. Laudatory obituaries appeared not only in motoring journals, or on petrolhead blogs, but in all of Britain's national newspapers. The most remarkable tribute came on television. It was delivered by the BBC – one of the handful of august British institutions, alongside things like the Wimbledon championships or a cricket test match at Lords, that had survived largely unchanged during John's lifetime. On the day following the formal announcement of his death, *Newsnight*, BBC television's flagship evening current affairs programme, ended its broadcast with an extraordinary gesture of recognition of the place he had come to occupy in Britain's popular culture. 'Motor manual founder John Haynes, who sold more than two hundred million copies of his "How to Fix It" books – has died,' the presenter began. 'It's said that he deconstructed everything and put it back to together again to create the books ... Here is our tribute.' Over the closing credits, they then ran a Haynes Manual breakdown of the *Newsnight* production studio.

Still the voices that would have meant most to Haynes himself came from ordinary car-owners young and old, from dozens of countries, whose lives he had touched. Hundreds upon hundreds of messages flooded into the Facebook pages of the museum and publishing group. Some were clearly a first gut reaction to hearing or reading the news that John Haynes was gone. They were the terse, digital equivalent of the kind of remark you'd have made, in an earlier age, to your husband or wife, or to a friend at the pub: 'Legend'... 'An icon'... 'A British national treasure'... or 'Damn! Not many people can say they've set the standard. RIP.'

Others recalled the place that Haynes's motor manuals had played in their own or their families' lives, and more than a few of them were directed toward the absent Haynes himself – a man with whom they had come to feel a sense of friendship, kinship almost, through his manuals. One, from a man named Anthony Clarke, said: 'Thank you for the memories of me and my dad changing the engine on my Chevette with your manual.' And from Sonja Mack: 'I remember my late husband using his Haynes manuals many a time on our battered second-hand cars. A life-saver. Kept us moving.' A man named Mark Michael Dance reminisced about the days 'before the age of the Internet, when Haynes manuals were my lifetime, and often my bedtime reading… sometimes for cars I didn't even own!' A man named David Harward called Haynes 'a legend, who helped me as a child,' adding, 'Now my children love your museum.'

There was Peter Dix, who wrote: 'My passion, my obsession, my love of cars started with the purchase of a simple Haynes manual, which quickly became the bible of my life, giving me the knowledge to support and fuel my determination and build my dreams. Thank you, John.' And movingly, from Patrick Carrube: 'My 14-year-old self, working in the cold nights of north-eastern Pennsylvania, fixing up a '78 Ram Charger. Thanks for all your efforts over the years.'

A man named Bobby Van Der Merwe, from the southern end of Africa, thanked Haynes for being his 'mentor and true inspiration… The reason I'm starting a transport museum in Zambia'. So far, he added, he had acquired a collection of thirty-odd vehicles, which he surely knew was very nearly the number with which John had started the museum in Sparkford.

There was a dash of fond good humour as well. 'You always knew – if a car that you bought had a Haynes Manual inside – just what part had been replaced. That was the page covered in oil. RIP, fella.' Another proclaimed John as 'the creator of the paper cut'. A man named Brett Coxon joked: 'Well, that's the world f**ked now: lads going around putting brake pads on the wrong way and everything.'

And there were also send-offs for John Haynes's final journey.

'RIP. You are responsible for more grazed knuckles than any person in history.'

'Rest in Peace, Mr Haynes. I hope you find a place in heaven, showing St Peter how to fix that old Bentley.'

# ACKNOWLEDGEMENTS

This is not an authorised biography, which makes the generosity shown to me by John Haynes's immediate family all the more extraordinary. I am immensely grateful to Annette, J, Chris and David Haynes. Without their insights and recollections, their willingness to give me so many hours of their time, and their superhuman patience in the face of what must at times have seemed an endless train of questions, this book quite simply could not have been written. I thank all of them for that – and thank them, too, for the gift of having met and got to know them.

I did not know John Haynes, but I do know someone who knew him well, and who persuaded me to write this book. Eddie Bell, the former HarperCollins chairman whom John brought onto his board and who went on to chair Haynes Publishing, happens to be my own long-time literary agent. Much more than that, he is a long-time, long-cherished, friend.

He was not my agent for this project, given his Haynes Publishing role, but I could not have asked for a better one: Eddie's gifted, astute and unfailingly supportive daughter, Jo, from the Bell Lomax Moreton Agency.

One of the pleasures in writing this book was discovering that John Haynes's life was a lot more complex, a lot richer, than his public persona suggested. In retracing his footsteps, and following the twists and turns he took before becoming the Haynes Manual Man, I benefited from the assistance of some truly extraordinary tour guides.

David, John's brother, was invaluable in sharing his memories of their childhood in Ceylon. David Colin-Thomé, the editor of a remarkable website called The History of Ceylon Tea, helped me trace the life and tea-plantation career of John's father, Harold Haynes.

Hugh and Judi Mayes were equally essential, and generous, in helping me tell the story of John's years at RAF Bruggen in Germany. David Hyland, owner of the famous Frogeye Sprite that was the subject of the first true Haynes Manual, generously shared his memories of their time together at RAF Khormaksar in Aden. Another indispensable guide to the years in Khormaksar was John's second in command there, David Welsh.

Many others helped with the other stages in John Haynes's life, and the many facets of his character.

Andrew 'AJ' Jeans shared his delightful memories as a fellow hill-climb and speed racer – and party animal – alongside John in the 1970s and '80s. Jane Marshall, whose Oxford Illustrated Press was one of his first book-publishing purchases, shared her memories of working with and for John, and of her long and continuing friendship with his family. Mike Penn, who helped John in creating the motor museum, was unfailingly, delightfully generous in providing his recollections of how the museum began, how its ever-expanding collection was assembled, and of how John, Annette, J, Marc and Chris contributed to making it what it is today.

The story of John's life could not be fully told without telling the story of the business that he created. Fortunately, I had an enormous head-start: a wonderfully detailed, and wonderfully readable, book released in 2000: *Haynes Publishing – The First Fifty Years*. But some of his other colleagues, including Murray

Corfield, helped round out the picture with their first-hand recollections.

But two people in particular were uniquely placed to allow me to cover the whole arc of John Haynes's extraordinary life. I've thanked them already, but want to add a special note of gratitude. The first is John's brother, David Haynes, who grew up with him in Ceylon; shared his years at Sutton Valence school in Kent; served, as John did, in the RAF; printed some of his first motor manuals; and returned as company secretary at Haynes Publishing for nearly two decades.

And there is Annette. She not only shared John's life for more than half a century, but she was an indispensable part of his life. He could not have flourished as a person, nor succeeded as a businessman, without her. She was kind and patient throughout the writing of this book. In helping me tell the story of what John achieved – and of who John was – she was always insightful, sometimes incisive, frequently funny, and of unfailingly good cheer.

Finally, no book gets published without the people who make sure it gets written on time, put together properly, presented and designed and distributed compellingly – all things that mere authors couldn't possibly get right. So I owe a special note of thanks to Louise McIntyre and Jeremy Yates-Round, supremos in the publishing department at Haynes.

# INDEX